Following Jesus in a Culture of FEAR

CHRISTIAN PRACTICE OF EVERYDAY LIFE

Scott Bader-Saye

BrazosPress
Grand Rapids, Michigan

Published by Brazos Press
a division of Baker Publishing Group
P.O. Box 6287, Grand Rapids, MI 49516-6287
www.brazospress.com

Printed in the United States of America

Library of Congress Cataloging-in-Publication Data
Bader-Saye, Scott
    Following Jesus in a culture of fear / Scott Bader-Saye
        p. cm. — (The Christian practice of everyday life)
    Includes bibliographical references.
    ISBN 10: 1-58743-192-0 (pbk.)
    ISBN 978-1-58743-192-0 (pbk.)
    1. Fear—Religious aspects—Christianity. 2. Christianity and culture. 3. Providence and government of God—Christianity. 4. Christian life. I. Title. II. Series
    BV4908.5.B33 2007
    248.4—dc22   2006101733

To Demery
Who taught my heart not to fear
and whose presence in my life
is a sure sign of God's providence

Contents

Acknowledgments

■ Thanks to the many people and institutions who helped make this book possible. First, thanks to the Louisville Institute, whose Christian Faith and Life Sabbatical Grant provided significant time and funding for research and conversation. Thanks also to the Institute staff and my fellow grantees who provided helpful feedback on early drafts of these ideas. I am grateful to the Passionist Nuns of St. Gabriel's Retreat Center in Clarks Summit, Pennsylvania, for providing a peaceful space to work during my sabbatical. Thanks to those who read and commented on drafts of chapters: Raymond Barfield, Pauline Palko, Mary Reed, Dan Shenk-Evans, Alice Townley, and Allison Treat. Your insights and suggestions saved me from many moments of "professor-speak" and helped make the final draft clearer and more accessible. I owe a debt to those who allowed me to use their personal stories as examples of living honestly and well in a culture of fear: Kate Brennan, Maureen Fiordimondo, Ollie and Heather Wagner, Bob Fox, and David Daily. Your lives of faith are an encouragement to me. Thanks to my editors at Brazos Press, Rodney Clapp and Rebecca Cooper, whose suggestions and support made this a better book. Thanks to the *Journal of the Society of Christian Ethics* for permission to reprint portions of "Thomas Aquinas and the Culture of Fear" (25:2, Fall/Winter 2005) in chapter 4.

My biggest thanks goes to my family—to Nolan, Eli, and Luke, who bring me joy and give me eyes to see, and to my wife, Demery, whose unflagging support kept me writing and whose superb editorial skill contributed to the text in countless ways.

Most loving Father, whose will it is for us to give thanks for all things, to fear nothing but the loss of you, and to cast all our care on you who cares for us: Preserve us from faithless fears and worldly anxieties, that no clouds of this mortal life may hide from us the light of that love which is immortal, and which you have manifested to us in your Son Jesus Christ our Lord; who lives and reigns with you, in the unity of the Holy Spirit, one God, now and for ever. *Amen.*

Collect for the Eighth Sunday after Epiphany
Episcopal Book of Common Prayer

1

Fear for Profit

■ *Do not be afraid.* We live in a time when this biblical refrain cannot be repeated too often. Both John Paul II in 1978 and his successor, Benedict XVI, in 2005 used these words to begin their papacies. Among all the things the church has to say to the world today, this may be the most important. No one has to be convinced that we live in fearful times, though we are not always sure what we should be afraid of and why. We suspect that our fears make us vulnerable to manipulation, but we find it hard to quell the fear long enough to analyze how it is being produced and directed for the benefit of others.

In the wake of the 9/11 terrorist attacks, the theme of fear has emerged in a variety of ways in popular culture, one of the most interesting being the 2004 CD from U2, *How to Dismantle an Atomic Bomb*. Bono, the rock star activist of U2, calls this album a journey from fear to faith. The disc begins with a track called "Vertigo." In an interview about the album, Bono describes vertigo as "a dizzy feeling, a sick feeling, when you get up to the top of something and there's only one way to go." He continues, "And in my head I created a club called Vertigo with all these people in it and the music is not the music you want to hear and the people are not the people you want to be with. . . . And then you just see somebody and she's got a cross around her neck, and you focus on it—because you can't focus on anything else. You find a little tiny fragment of salvation there."[1]

In the song, Bono describes this vertiginous fear as "everything I wish I didn't know," as a place where your head is a "jungle," where "bullets rip the sky" and fear holds you in "check mate." Toward the end of the song this fear morphs into temptation, and Vertigo makes a devilish offer, not unlike the deal Satan offered to Jesus in the wilderness. Bono repeats three times the words "All of this can be yours," echoing Jesus's three temptations, and ends with an offer that promises false security, "Just give me what I want and no one gets hurt." Vertigo tempts us to take power, the wrong kind of power, in order to free ourselves from fear's bondage. But the song hints at another option: "the girl with crimson nails / has Jesus round her neck," and it ends with Bono singing, "Your love is teaching me how to kneel." The album as a whole moves toward this place of kneeling, this place of faith, and the last track, "Yahweh," offers a prayer, "take this heart and make it break." The path out of fear is not power but trust, not strength but vulnerability before God. Unfortunately, it is easy to lose sight of this in a culture that is at once confused about the goods we should seek and ready to exploit our resulting anxieties for profit.

Fearful Parenting

My wife and I discovered that we had not yet begun to know fear until we had our first child. Eager to master this new challenge, we took to the books soon after learning Demery was pregnant. From *What to Expect When You're Expecting* to Bradley's *Husband-Coached Childbirth,* we investigated what the experts were saying. We quickly realized we were in territory littered with land mines. From pregnancy to parenting, we wanted to do the right thing in a situation where it was no longer self-evident what the "right thing" was. Should we reclaim the practice of a simpler time and have the baby at home with a midwife? Should we hire a doula to assist my wife and attend to her comfort? Should we take advantage of the full medical and technological capacities of the modern hospital, trusting ourselves to well-trained doctors and nurses? If so, should we allow the doctors to give medications that might facilitate a quicker, less painful birth? Then again, such drugs might lengthen labor and be dangerous for the baby. How would we know? The uncertainty quickly turned to fear that we might make the wrong decision for our child.

Where once it was enough to listen to the wisdom handed down from one mother to the next, it had become important to consult an array of "experts" in order to be a responsible parent. But while the modern world had taught us to trust the professionals and to distrust hand-me-down advice, our postmodern ethos had taught us that even the expert opinion is not immune to overstatement, blind spots, and self-interest. So where did that leave us? We were too savvy to go back to Mom and Grandma and ask them how to raise our children. Yet neither could we pull a copy of Dr. Spock or Dr. Sears off the shelf and trust that this expert had properly and sufficiently mapped the terrain of childbirth and parenting.

Parenting is increasingly an arena of fear and anxiety in part because family life in general now lacks any cultural consensus about norms and standards. It's not just that we don't know if we're "getting it right," but that we don't even know what "right" would look like. And while experts-in-the-field can be very helpful in certain cases (for instance, I'm very happy to go to a medical expert when my child is sick), when the experts disagree we are left with an uncertainty that only magnifies our fear.

In the absence of agreement about "good parenting," we increasingly find solace in "safe parenting." We don't let the nurses take our baby to the hospital nursery, because we've heard stories of babies getting mixed up or even stolen. Sure, it's unlikely, but it happens—we saw it on *Dateline*! And what about vaccinations? Don't they sometimes backfire and produce the very disease they are trying to prevent? Wasn't there a Miss America candidate who was permanently injured by a vaccination? We baby-proof (what an odd term) the house with all the latest safety products—outlets covered, gates installed, furniture attached to the wall, protective padding placed on all sharp corners, plastic guard secured on the stove, drawers locked, crib inspected, toilets latched. Ordinary living becomes fraught with reminders of extraordinary dangers.

Even sleeping poses a threat. How many parents have awoken in the night to make sure their baby was still breathing? The SIDS (Sudden Infant Death Syndrome) awareness campaign has undoubtedly done good things, but it has also extended our fearfulness into a time when we should find rest. And, as Frank Furedi, a sociologist at the University of Kent, notes, "the relentless publicity that surrounds crib death produces anxieties that are completely disproportionate to the scale of the problem."[2] The SIDS rate has fallen by over 50 percent since 1983, down to about 2,500 deaths per year in the United States, out of approximately 4 million births.[3] The SIDS Institute describes the syndrome as "very rare," yet for many parents the anxiety about SIDS far exceeds its likelihood. Of course, raising awareness is not a bad thing, but parents need to know how to place the SIDS danger in a context that allows them to sleep well at night and avoid inordinate fear.

In the midst of all these parenting fears, the marketplace steps forward ready to offer solutions—for a price. Child safety has become a lucrative industry in part because legitimate fears are artificially heightened and manipulated. When "good parenting" is replaced by "safe parenting," child rearing is easily captured by consumption—we may not be able to buy goodness, but we can buy safety. And if a given product claims to make your child safer, how do you refrain from buying it without seeming to say, "I'm not interested in my child's safety." Yet where does it end? Being locked in a padded room is very safe, but it's hardly a life.

The wonderful animated movie *Finding Nemo* explores themes of risk, safety, and the limits of parental control. Having lost his wife and a nestful of eggs to a shark attack, the clownfish Marlin makes it his mission to preserve his only remaining child, Nemo, from all danger. At one point he says to his friend Dory: "I promised him I'd never let anything happen to him." To which Dory replies, "Huh. That's a funny thing to promise." "What?" "Well, you can't '*never* let anything happen to him.' Then nothing would ever happen to him. Not much fun for little [Nemo]."[4] At some point our preoccupation with safety can get in the way of living full lives. Fear can poison a host of good and life-giving activities that we once took for granted, like taking a walk in the woods, playing in the sun, or swimming in the ocean.

What happens when we parent out of fear? We begin thinking primarily about what we want to prevent and avoid rather than what we want to encourage and develop. We direct our energy toward a minimalist credo: "allow no harm." But it is not enough to keep our children safe. Their physical safety is a backdrop against which we as parents need to help them discover the joy of living, the thrill of new experiences, a robust engagement with the world around them, a dynamic relationship with the God who made them. All of this can easily be squelched when we parent out of fear. Parents need to create space for our children to explore and even take risks in the process of growing, learning, and developing. We want our children to grow into adults who are expansive and generous rather than fearful and constricted, yet the culture of fear routinely squelches such an extravagant embrace of life.

Marketing, Media, and Fear

The fears associated with childhood and parenting are only one small subset of the broader cultural anxiety that assails us. Fear has long been a profitable handmaid for marketers and news agencies. When *Newsweek* publishes an article entitled, "That Little Freckle Could Be a Time Bomb,"[5] and when local news anchors lead into stories with the words: "Why drinking too much water could send you to the emergency room,"[6] we can be sure that fear has become a bottom-line issue. We are surrounded by fear just to the extent that we are surrounded by people who profit from fear.

This may help explain why our fears do not often correspond to our actual level of risk. For instance, Furedi observes, "far more people die from an inadequate diet than from the widely publicized presence of toxic residues in food. . . . Clearly, the risks that kill you are not necessarily the ones that provoke and frighten you."[7] According to the Center for Disease Control, the top three causes of death in the United States in 2002 were, in order, heart disease, cancer, and stroke.[8] Yet these are not what we are afraid of, at least not in the same way we are afraid of terrorism, pedophiles, road rage, school shootings, plane wrecks, risky strangers, monster moms, killer bees, serial killers, new addictions (including shopping addiction and Internet addiction syndrome), and a host of new medical and psychological conditions (such as mad cow disease, attention-deficit hyperactivity disorder, and super-viruses such as West Nile, SARS, bird flu, and Ebola).[9]

Although we may be experiencing a heightened level of fear and insecurity, the truth is that our world is no more dangerous now than 50 years ago, 100 years ago, or 1,000 years ago. The types of dangers have changed—no one had to worry about plane crashes a hundred years ago—but in general we (at least "we" in the West) are living longer, healthier lives than ever before. Consider how many serious illnesses, such as polio, measles, and smallpox, have been eradicated or diminished in developed countries in the last century. Those who think air travel has increased our risk should consider the hardships and dangers associated with traveling long distances by horse and buggy. Those who think youth are more violent today than ever should know that in 1850 New York City recorded over two hundred gang wars, most fought by adolescent boys (viewing the movie *Gangs of New York* will visually drive the point home, even if the violence is somewhat exaggerated).[10] Youth violence is not new. Dangerous travel is not new. Our present dangers are for the most part perennial dangers. Yet in many ways we imagine ourselves to be more threatened than ever.

In the 1990s crime rates were dropping while two-thirds of Americans believed they were rising.[11] What accounts for this perception? One possible answer is what George Gerbner, dean emeritus of the Annenberg School of Communication at the University of Pennsylvania, has called the "mean world syndrome." In his years of research on television violence, he has found not so much a direct link between TV violence and real-world violence as a link between TV violence and exaggerated fearfulness. Because we witness so much brutality, both on TV dramas and news programs, we come to believe that the world is a scary and ominous place filled with violent predators. Gerbner found that "people who watch a lot of TV are more likely than others to believe their neighborhoods are unsafe, to assume that crime rates are rising, and to overestimate their own odds of becoming a victim."[12] They are also more likely to own guns.[13] Indeed it seems that the real effect of viewing TV violence is not a direct tendency to become violent (though that may be the indirect result) as much as a propensity to become fearful.

Another reason we are a more fearful culture today, despite the fact that the dangers are not objectively greater than in the past, is because some people have incentives and means to heighten, manipulate, and exploit our fears. Fear is a strong motivator, and so those who want and need to motivate others—politicians, advertisers, media executives, advocacy groups, even the church—turn to fear to bolster their message. I call this the "fear for profit" syndrome, and it is rampant. We have become preoccupied with unlikely dangers that take on the status of imminent threats, producing a culture where fear determines a disproportionate number of our personal and communal decisions. The sense of ever-increasing threats can overwhelm our ability to evaluate and respond proportionately to each new risk; thus, we allow fear to overdetermine our actions.

TV news and news magazines bombard us with a certain kind of fear-mongering that follows a distinct pattern. First, they present a hyped-up teaser, usually a variation on the "what you don't know might kill you" theme. "Coming up next, the story of a man who [fill in sensational catastrophe]. Find out how you can avoid becoming the next victim." Beginning with the story of a shocking "real-life" catastrophe (sometimes reenacted to give us a visual image of the danger), these stories continue by discussing this danger with a few "specialists" and end with helpful "tips" about how the rest of us can avoid this horrible fate. Consider the episode of *20/20* that examined the problem of patients catching fire on the operating table when a surgical instrument ignites oxygen from a face mask.[14] The very thought of this causes our anxiety levels to rise, and seeing the scarred face of just one victim magnifies our fear. The story gives the impression that this is a danger that could happen to any of us, yet this tragedy happens only once out of every 270,000 surgeries (about .0004 percent of the time). The likelihood of this happening is minuscule, yet we are told by Barbara Walters that this happens "more often than you might think"—a claim that seems frightening and is probably true but only because most of us were unaware that it happened at all.[15] The story creates a false sense of danger as a way of marketing the program.

Why do marketers and the media like to stir up fear? Fear, like sex, is one of our basic instincts, a primal reaction. Both fear and lust move us to act; just as "sex sells," so does fear. If marketers can tap into our fear, they can sell us a product to calm that fear, whether the product is a news story (profiting through advertising) or an alarm system. Recently, Al Franken responded to the charges that the news media has either a liberal or a conservative bias (depending on who is making the charge) by noting that there is another media bias that we should be much more concerned about—the profit-making bias.[16] This bias affects both the selection of news stories and the angle of coverage.

We will better understand the need for news to make a profit if we take a quick look at the history of the news business in the United States. When broadcasting began in the 1930s, the United States government allowed for-profit companies to control the public airwaves.[17] There was no U.S. equivalent to Britain's non-profit BBC (British Broadcasting Corporation). In return for using a public resource (the airwaves) for making a private profit, these companies had to show that they were providing a "public service." The FCC could challenge the license of any broadcaster on the basis of its public service record. Broadcasters were happy to show that they were losing money on news as a form of public service (while making loads of money through their other divisions), thus defending against any FCC challenge. But with the deregulation of broadcasting that began in the 1980s, "the FCC largely abandoned the practice of challenging licenses on public service grounds."[18] The rise of competition from cable companies further contributed to the demand that network news shows not lose money. We have seen, therefore, the rapid expansion of news-for-profit in the last twenty years. Corporate owners of the news companies hire consulting firms to conduct surveys and do market research to determine what concerns viewers and ultimately what will boost ratings. The results are passed along to the news divisions, who are told, as one executive put it, "what they ought to be covering and how they ought to be covering it."[19] News that is driven by a profit motive has to have ratings that can create advertising revenue. This is increasingly achieved through disproportionate coverage of the sensational and the shocking, which only intensifies our sense of fear.

Of course, not all of our fears have to do with death and loss. We also fear failure and rejection. These fears haunt our personal relationships and our work lives. Women, especially, are targeted by advertising strategies that depict unrealistic images of beauty, suggest that the viewer or reader does not match up, and then offer to sell a product that will relieve her fear of inadequacy: buy this magazine with ten beauty/sex/relationship/hair tips, or you will be relegated to "ordinary"; buy this deodorant, or face the embarrassment of body odor. Likewise, men are told to buy this acne medication, or you will be just another loser; buy this car, or you will not appear successful. Marketers excel at the creation and manipulation of what is "cool," "hip," and "sexy," and in so doing they tap into our fears of rejection and failure. I recently saw an advertisement in *Rolling Stone* magazine declaring "No Lame Ring Tones" and featuring a beautiful woman holding out her cell phone. Of course, for a small price you, too, can get a ring tone that will rescue you from your pathetic lameness.

Terrorism, Politics, and Fear

All of the fears discussed here so far pale before the vast, fear-producing experience of September 11, 2001. The terrorist attacks on the United States produced a new level of anxiety and vulnerability that shocked Americans out of their "it could never happen here" mentality. After the initial experience of astonishment and grief, fear morphed into anger, and the nation quickly became caught up in the rhetoric of revenge. These attacks gave a face to our deepest fears, and though the probability of dying in a terrorist attack on American soil was still incredibly low, the horrific magnitude of these acts allowed them to produce a pervasive anxiety that extended far beyond the actual threat.

The events of 9/11 not only have reshaped American political discourse, but have, unfortunately, provided new opportunities to exploit fear to gain political capital. Many have suggested that the Bush administration used the 9/11 strikes as an excuse to pursue initiatives, both foreign and domestic, that were already on the agenda but would have lacked public support apart from such a crisis.

For instance, ousting Saddam Hussein seems to have been a goal for some in the Bush administration even prior to 9/11.[20] After the attacks, the administration seized the opportunity to invade Iraq despite the fact that Iraq was never directly linked to the hijackings. In his 2003 State of the Union address, Bush made the case for war, implying a connection between Saddam Hussein and 9/11, even though the White House admitted that they had discovered nothing to link Hussein to the attacks: "Before September the 11th, many in the world believed that Saddam Hussein could be contained. But chemical agents, lethal viruses and shadowy terrorist networks are not easily contained. Imagine those 19 hijackers with other weapons and other plans—this time armed by Saddam Hussein. It would take one vial, one canister, one crate slipped into this country to bring a day of horror like none we have ever known. We will do everything in our power to make sure that that day never comes."[21] If September 11 shows that Saddam Hussein could be contained, the obvious conclusion is that Hussein was somehow involved (thus, not contained) on September 11. By all accounts, however, this is not true.[22] Bush made this explicit when he admitted in a statement in September 2003, "We've had no evidence that Saddam Hussein was involved with September the 11th."[23] But by linking the public fear surrounding 9/11 to Saddam Hussein, Bush was able to garner public support by transferring our generalized fear of terror to a specific enemy who, as it turned out, had no real capacity to threaten the United States.

Of course, manipulating fears to pursue a partisan agenda hardly qualifies as a new political practice, and both parties in U.S. politics have proven themselves capable of such tactics. Indeed, the presidential campaign of 2004 was nothing if not a fear-fest. Each party dressed itself in flag and uniform and portrayed the other party as dangerous. The Democrats were painted with the "soft-on-terror" brush, while the Republicans were decried as "reckless unilateralists." The moral of the campaign: if you can't woo voters, scare them. For a time, it seemed that the entire arena of political conversation was reduced to the topic of security, the new alpha issue of single-issue politics.

During his speech at the Democratic National Convention that year, Bill Clinton proclaimed, "Now, their opponents will tell you we should be afraid of John Kerry and John Edwards because they won't stand up to the terror. Don't you believe it. Strength and wisdom are not opposing values. They go hand in hand. They go hand in hand, and John Kerry has both. His first priority will be to keep America safe. Remember the scripture, 'Be not afraid.'"[24] Clinton smoothly draws upon the Bible to make his political claim, but in so doing he implies that overcoming fear has more to do with electing John Kerry president than with, say, trusting in God. Apparently, most Americans didn't believe him.

The notorious elect-Dukakis-and-murderers-like-Willie-Horton-will-roam-the-streets ads during the 1988 campaign famously exploited fear to bolster the elder Bush's presidential run. The fear of crime has long been a mainstay of political campaigning, even when crime rates were dropping and other issues were far more pressing. For example, in my quiet, relatively crime-free town in northeastern Pennsylvania, election time brings a *Fear-Factor*-style media blitz. As the first Tuesday of November approaches, a spate of television commercials warns senior citizens about the dangers of crime. The candidates promise to protect seniors through "harsh sentencing" of offenders. The fact that seniors are being targeted by this ad is a bit odd, since recent Justice Department reports show that "people over sixty-five are less likely than any other age group to become victims of violent crime."[25] The actual threat does not correspond to the advertising hype, yet the real point is clear: seniors vote, and this kind of political advertising seeks to mobilize seniors based on misrepresentations of their peril.

Fear in Church

To be fair, we have to add one more group to the list of those who use fear to consolidate power and influence opinion—religious leaders. As Paul Marshall, Bishop of the Episcopal Diocese of Bethlehem, observes, "When others want power, or when they want to get people to do their will, they play to our fears. 'There's trouble in River City,' was how the Music Man got people to buy his goods. Religious groups are particularly vulnerable to the kind of demagoguery that creates and capitalizes on fear. Many private religious empires in America have been built by religious entrepreneurs who play to people's fears. The airwaves are full of them."[26] Indeed, the fear of hell and fear of the sword have long been favorite tools of evangelism. The conquistadores notoriously converted indigenous peoples in Central and South America at swordpoint, and evangelists in the revivalist tradition have made ample use of hell to scare people into heaven.

I recently stumbled on a website selling "Fear God" T-shirts and pro-moting "shirt evangelism."[27] The website boasts: "The Fear God line of shirts contains bold scriptural truths. You won't be able to wear one of these shirts without telling someone about Jesus!" The shirts tout such fear-mongering slogans as "He Ain't Coming Back to Preach—Fear God," featuring a line-drawn image of a man on horseback brandishing a sword. And who could pass up the "It Is a Dreadful Thing to Fall into the Hands of the Living God: Repent or Perish" T-shirt sporting a skull with "666" imprinted on the forehead. The shirt company informs us that this quality shirt "shows the remains of a person who went through the judgment of God almighty." Ironically, the website suggests that wearing these shirts will be an easy way to draw "the lost" into conversations about God, because "people are more willing to listen when they are not threatened"! One could only wish that this site were a satire, but instead it reflects the worst melding of Christianity and the market—using fear to gain religious profit and financial profit at the same time (T-shirts can be purchased for $14.95).

Of course, there are other, subtler forms of religious fear-mongering. In many ways the Christian subculture of books, music, concerts, festivals, schools, kitsch, and clothing depends on creating a subculture of fear. Spencer Burke, a pastor who speaks and blogs about church and culture, explains: "Believing that the world is an evil place to raise our children, we take a variety of steps to insulate ourselves from that reality. We watch Christian videos, read Christian books, and listen to Christian music. Why? Because we deem these items to be 'safe.'"[28] Some Christians would rather retreat to the safety of a Christ-saturated subculture than live in a com-plex, gray-shaded world.[29] The new trend among Christian radio stations is to describe themselves as "safe for the whole family," a description tailored to calm fearful listeners but hardly reflective of the Jesus who says dangerous things like "take up your cross and follow me."

The irony is that this Christian subculture reproduces secular culture at its most problematic level: its commitment to defining all life choices as consumer choices. As we have seen, fear often drives consumption in the hope that some new product will make us just a little safer. Christian marketing exploits the same manipulative practices, suggesting that a particular product or a style of consuming will make us feel safer. "Christian" then becomes more a description of certain kinds of "safe" products than a description of a people. We pretend to risk engagement with the world by mimicking the culture's trends in music, fashion, and technology, when all we are really doing is covering the rough edges of real life with a smooth coat of Jesus.

I suspect that much of the allure of the *Left Behind* series of books and movies has to do with its exploitation of fear. This happens at a number of levels. There is, first, our fear of the apocalypse understood as a violent and cataclysmic end of the world. This fear is, thankfully, calmed by the authors' view that the "rapture," that is, the raising up of all Christians to be with Christ in heaven, will happen before the "tribulation," that is, the time when all hell breaks loose on earth. Don't fear the orgy of violence ahead, these books tell us, because the "true" Christians will be spared. In addition, the series responds to Christian fear of a sinful world by celebrating the impending apocalyptic judgment. Fear not, the books tell us, non-Christians will get what they deserve. *Left Behind* addresses Christian fear but at the same time stokes that fear by describing in detail both the threatening sinfulness of the world and the awful judgment that will fall on those who do not believe.

This kind of Christian fear-mongering is not entirely new. Back in 1952 the Swiss theologian Hans Urs von Balthasar warned against giving in to apocalyptic fear. "The Word of God guarantees an objective distance from those Christian prophets of doom, who apply their misplaced melancholy and radicalism to the task of announcing the immediate and total demise of everything that is of lasting importance in the Church today."[30] We need a similar kind of "objective distance" from those in the church who would use fear to manipulate conversions or to shore up a triumphalist but fearful Christian subculture.

Politicians, the media, advertisers, even religious leaders, have a profit motive for exacerbating and sustaining our fears. This profit may come in the form of money, viewership, filled pews, influence, or power, but in each case we are encouraged to fear the wrong things or to fear the right things in the wrong way. Our anxiety, then, drives us to act in ways that override other moral concerns. We spend our money based on fear rather than stewardship. We make political decisions based on fear rather than the common good. We participate in religious life based on fear rather than love.

Following Jesus

We are in need of some clear, sensible reflection on fear—how to acknowledge it without being manipulated by it, how to resist it without assuming we should (or could) be fearless, how to receive it as a gift (if it can be a gift) without letting it dominate our lives. This is especially important among Christians who seek to follow Jesus, for Jesus's words, and more so his life, do not promise safety. Following the teachings of Jesus will involve us in risky practices like clothing the naked, visiting the prisoner, caring for the sick, welcoming the stranger, and feeding the hungry (see Matt. 25:31–46). Following the life of Jesus will mean walking in the way of the cross, the way of "self-giving love."[31] The apostle Paul describes this vocation in his second letter to the Corinthians, "For while we live, we are always being given up to death for Jesus' sake, so that the life of Jesus may be made visible in our mortal flesh" (2 Cor. 4:11). Such risky discipleship can hardly be described as "safe."

Of course, we have to be careful not to glorify risk, suffering, or powerlessness in a way that simply reinforces oppression. As Richard Hays cautions, "The image of the cross should not be used by those who hold power in order to ensure the acquiescent suffering of the powerless. Instead, the New Testament insists that *the community as a whole* is called to follow in the way of Jesus' suffering. The New Testament writers consistently employ the pattern of the cross precisely to call those who possess power and privilege to *surrender* it for the sake of the weak."[32] Christian discipleship, that is, following Jesus, will mean surrendering the power that masquerades as security in order to love the neighbor and welcome the stranger. It will mean avoiding the safe path in order to pursue the good. But in a culture of fear, we find such risks all the more difficult, since our natural inclinations lead us to close in on ourselves when we face danger. How can we maintain the posture of the open hand toward a world that scares us? The following chapters will, hopefully, provide resources for living into the joyful freedom of those children of God who have learned to put fear in its place.

Questions for Discussion

1. Can you think of any examples of advertisements, political commercials, or news stories that create and manipulate fear? Do you think they work? If so, why do they work?
2. From your perspective as a child and/or parent, how has fear shaped your family life? Do you have memories of being taught to fear as a child? If so, do you think these fears taught you to live with proper care, or did they distort your view of the world?
3. George Gerbner claims that too much TV creates a "mean world syndrome." Does this seem true of your experience or that of people you know?

4. Make a list of things you fear. Which ones would you describe as legitimate fears, that is, fears that help you avoid actual, present dangers? Which fears would you describe as constructed or manipulated fears, that is, fears that arise not from a significant threat but from some outside source (media, religion, politics) that wants to profit from your fear?

5. How can we avoid being manipulated by fear-mongering? What tactics of resistance might we employ to ward off the fearful messages we receive every day?

6. The church has at times used fear of hell as a means of evangelism ("believe in Jesus, or go to hell") and as a way of keeping its members morally upright ("avoid sin, or you will go to hell"). Do you think this is a legitimate use of fear? How might we address the temptation of the church to use fear to control or manipulate?

7. How do you think Jesus wants us to respond to fear? Why does Jesus ask us to do things that might make us vulnerable or afraid? Can you think of any stories in the Gospels in which Jesus addresses the fears of his followers? What might these stories teach us about fear?

2

Fear and the Moral Life

■ So if we do, in fact, live in a culture of fear, what does all of this fear do to us? What kind of people do we become if we are fed a steady diet of dread? More specifically, how does fear affect our moral lives?

Perhaps the place to begin answering this is with a very basic question: why speak of fear as a *moral* issue at all? Isn't it the case that fear is an emotion, and if so, how can we say that feeling an emotion is good or bad? We don't experience our emotions (or what the ancients called our "passions") as chosen but as simply arising from within or washing over us. Popular wisdom will tell us, "Your feelings are not good or bad, they're just feelings." How, then, can we speak of them as being appropriate or inappropriate, moral or immoral?

Theologian Simon Harak gives examples that help us recognize that emotions are anything but neutral. "It is somehow wrong," he observes, "not to feel revulsion at rape, or to stay forever angry with imperfect parents. It is somehow right to rejoice at a friend's success, or to be moved by the plight of an abused child. So it seems upon reflection that our passions can be morally praise- or blameworthy."[1] The Christian tradition of character formation tells us that the proper ordering of our passions (including fear) is part of what shapes character. If, for instance, we wish to develop the virtues of courage and hope, we need to learn what to fear and how much to fear it. But we can do this only when we recognize that our emotional responses are, themselves, largely socially conditioned.

25

Though the capacity to fear may be innate, the specifics of what we fear, when we fear, and how much we fear are largely learned. Scientific studies have shown this to be true in other animals; for instance, if a mother rat is made to be fearful and anxious during pregnancy, the baby rats will exhibit fearful and anxious behavior as well. And if new babies are introduced to this fearful mother, they too will begin to exhibit fear behavior.[2] These studies lend credence to what Christians have long believed to be true, that our passions are not just given but are formed. Thus, we can be shaped to feel the passions in the right way, at the right time, and to the right extent—to rejoice rightly at the triumph of the good, to lament rightly in the face of suffering, and to feel anger rightly in the presence of evil.

Fear is not evil. It is not a vice. It is not wrong to fear, but excessive or disordered fear can tempt us to vices such as cowardice, sloth, rage, and violence. It can also inhibit virtuous actions such as hospitality, peace-making, and generosity. Walter Brueggemann tells the story of Martin Niemöller, a German Lutheran pastor who courageously opposed Adolph Hitler at a time when many Christians were supporting him. As a young man in 1933, Niemöller met with Hitler "as part of a delegation of leaders of the Evangelical Lutheran Church. . . . Niemöller stood at the back of the room and looked and listened. He didn't say anything. When he went home, his wife asked him what he had learned that day. Niemöller replied, 'I discovered that Herr Hitler is a terribly frightened man.'"[3] While fear itself may not be evil, disordered fear can certainly create the opportunity and (apparent) justification for great evil.

Fear's Moral Options: Attack or Contract

Fear is a moral issue insofar as it shapes the kind of people we become, and the kind of people we become has a lot to do with how we see the world around us. Our judgments about what is going on in the world and how to interpret events go a long way toward helping us define proper actions. Quite simply, how we view (or interpret) the world shapes how we act in the world. The twentieth-century American ethicist H. Richard Niebuhr went so far as to say that the first question of ethics is not "What is right?" or even "What is good?" but rather "What is going on?"[4] Before we can apply a law or seek a goal, we must first interpret what is happening around us. Thus, reading the signs of the times is itself a moral act. In order to live well, we need to know how God is involved in history. To use Niebuhr's terms, the moral life is centered around the "fitting" response to the pattern of God's activity in the world.

26

But what if we are unable to see God's hand in our lives or in the world around us? What if history does not seem to be unfolding a divine purpose but only lurching this way and that in response to one crisis after another? What if, in a postmodern world, we are less likely to see a "story" in history and more likely to see randomness, chaos, and threat? Niebuhr seemed to recognize that for many it was becoming harder and harder to see God at work in the world. "We see ourselves surrounded by animosity," he writes, "Hence the color of our lives is anxiety and self-preservation is our first law."[5]

In a culture of fear, the short answer to "What is going on?" is "We are at risk" or "We are in danger." Insofar as we accept that answer as our dominant description of the world, our lives will be shaped by the self-preservation of which Niebuhr speaks. Our moral vision becomes tunnel vision. Fear becomes the ambient background to our lives rather than a proper response to a concrete and passing threat.

Psychologists tell us that fear in humans (as well as animals) tends to provoke one of two reactions: fight or flight. We either attack that which threatens us, hoping to overcome it, or we contract, withdrawing and fleeing from danger. On their 2001 CD, *The Places You Have Come to Fear the Most,* the alternative rock group Dashboard Confessional explores the ways in which ambient fear leads us to contract into ourselves. On the title track to the CD, singer and songwriter Chris Carrabba links fear and death:

> the grave that you refuse to leave
> the refuge that you've built to flee
> the places that you've come to fear the most
> is the place that you have come to fear the most.
> Buried deep as you can dig inside yourself
> and hidden in the public eye
> such a stellar monument to loneliness.[6]

Carrabba poignantly illumines the consequences of fear in these lyrics. He recognizes that once fears exceed their boundaries, they follow us even as we try to flee. This flight from fear, in turn, leads to a grave of loneliness that is even more frightening than our fears themselves. The answer to fear cannot be a retreat from love or a retreat from the world, though this is exactly what excessive fear tempts us to do. On another track, "This Ruined Puzzle," Carrabba further explores this theme, noting the irony that fear, which begins as self-preservation, ends as self-consumption:

> This basement's a coffin,
> I'm buried alive.
> I'll die in here just to be safe.[7]

Carrabba probably did not have the thirteenth-century theologian Thomas Aquinas in mind as he was writing these songs. Nonetheless, his description of the way we "dig inside ourselves" bears a close resemblance to what Aquinas refers to as the "contraction" that comes with fear. Aquinas writes that "fear arises from the imagination of some threatening evil which is difficult to repel. . . . But that a thing be difficult to repel is due to lack of power . . . and the weaker a power is, the fewer the things to which it extends. Wherefore from the very imagination that causes fear there ensues a certain contraction in the appetite."[8] That is to say, fear is produced, in part, by our judgment that we are not strong enough to fight off a threat. Lacking power, we contract, we withdraw into ourselves to conserve what strength and energy we have in order to fend off the danger. In this context Aquinas uses the Greek term *systolē*, from which we get our English term *systolic* (referring to the contracting of the heart muscle as it pumps blood into the arteries). Fear, for Aquinas, can cause a kind of contraction of the heart. By imagining some future evil, fear draws us in on ourselves so that we "extend" ourselves to "fewer things." This, in turn, becomes a hindrance to Christian discipleship, which calls us not to contract but to expand, not to limit ourselves to a few things but to open ourselves charitably and generously to many things, not to attack that which threatens us but to love even the enemy.

The Ethic of Safety

Fear tempts us to make safety and self-preservation our highest goals, and when we do so our moral focus becomes the protection of our lives and health. Security becomes the new idol before whom all other gods must bow. In the past, when asked "What is your chief goal?" Christians have given answers such as "friendship with God" (Thomas Aquinas) or "to glorify God and enjoy him forever" (Westminster Catechism, seventeenth century).[9] Today, I suspect many Christians would echo the culture in naming "safety" or "security" as the primary good they seek.

I was recently traveling by plane and found myself strangely attentive to the flight attendant's recitation of "the safety features of this aircraft." Among them are the oxygen masks that automatically drop down in the event of a loss of cabin pressure. Then I heard the familiar refrain: "If you are traveling with someone who needs assistance, first secure your own mask." I've heard it many times before, but this time I could not help but hear "first secure your own mask" as a kind of motto for the new ethic of safety. While I don't doubt this is useful advice in the event of an airline emergency, the assumption that we must secure our own safety before we can extend ourselves to others may not serve us well as followers of Jesus in a frightened and frightening world.

Frank Furedi has written extensively about the impact of fear on our social and political lives. Fear, he says, has "transform[ed] safety into one of the main virtues of society," making it an object of "worship."[10] He warns us, "The disposition to panic, the remarkable dread of strangers and the feebleness of relations of trust have all had important implications for everyday life. . . . The outcome of these developments is a world view which equates the good life with self-limitation and risk aversion."[11]

Disordered and excessive fear has significant moral consequences. It fosters a set of shadow virtues, including suspicion, preemption, and accumulation, which threaten traditional Christian virtues such as hospitality, peacemaking, and generosity. Thus, in an interesting way our preoccupation with safety provides a temporary, though artificial, solution to our moral fragmentation. We modern people may not be able to reach much agreement on the hard issues like abortion, capital punishment, war, health care, sex, and poverty. We may not agree on what virtues are most desirable for living a full human life. Indeed we may not even be able to agree on what a full human life looks like. But we can all agree on safety. The new ethic of safety provides a least-common-denominator morality—surely we can all agree that we don't want to die. Surely we can all agree that safety is of the utmost importance, since without life and health we cannot pursue any of the other greater goods. Our common fearfulness, then, takes on the appearance of a gift in that it creates a common goal—safety—among a populace otherwise fragmented by culture wars.

Such unity, however, is deceptive. When we were all gathered around our televisions watching the destruction on 9/11, we knew that we were at that moment gathered together in a common experience with all our fellow citizens and with sympathetic souls around the world. During the 2002 sniper attacks in Washington D.C., we shared a common fear with those who were threatened, even if we lived hundreds or thousands of miles away. In a strange way it made us one. The temptation, then, is to make something of this community built of fear, to prolong it, because as a fragmented people we want to linger in those moments when we share a corporate mind and heart. In the end, however, such a community cannot last. Living only to prevent destruction, we neglect the calling to construct, to build a common life and to seek common goods. We are tempted to settle for a minimalist and passive ethic that says simply "avoid pain," "stay safe," and "be careful."

One symptom of our new ethic of safety is that our moral language has been "medicalized." We have become increasingly worried about judging others, because we no longer have a common cache of expectations on which to draw for these judgments. So, in order to avoid offense, ethical claims are often justified by an appeal to safety rather than to morality or goodness. Furedi gives this example: "Instead of the old morality, which targeted the promiscuous single mother, the new etiquette attacks a pregnant woman for smoking or drinking alcohol and thereby placing her future child at risk."[12] Even if promiscuity is addressed, it is often in medical terms having to do with avoiding a disease or healing a "sex addiction." But by defining the relevant issues this way, our sexuality is no longer seen in terms of how it serves the good of God's creating and redeeming activity. It is seen instead in terms of how it serves the good of personal health and safety. Thus, the cultural purveyors of the new ethic of "safe = good" (from sex-education classes to MTV) tell young people that if they are going to have sex, at least have "safe sex." Not practicing "safe sex" is the new moral infraction.

This fear-based revision of our sexual ethic comes at the cost of a proper understanding of sex as a good gift that need not be feared. Sex belongs within marriage not because it is "risky" (or at least its risks are quite different when seen within the Christian story) but because it creates a physical unity that can be fully celebrated only in a context of spiritual unity. Sex belongs within marriage not because it is an intrinsically unsafe act but because we need the community of marriage to help us welcome and care for new life. Regulating sex through fear may produce the restraint that traditional moralists hope for but only at the cost of misunderstanding sex and reinforcing the idea that moral decisions have to do with safety rather than goodness or holiness.

Is it a bad thing to be healthy and safe? Certainly not. But Christians want to do more than just teach our young people to engage or not engage in certain behaviors. We want to teach them how to think about moral matters. Yet the message we are sending is that the proper standards for moral decision making are health, safety, and security. We fail to help them see sex as part of the great adventure (and risk) of living in a covenant that mirrors to the world the beauty and thrill of divine love. When we teach youth that what matters most is being safe and that abstinence is the only sure way to be safe, we may gain some ground in the battle against premarital sex, but at the cost of reinforcing an ethic of safety. Perhaps we fear that acknowledging the joy and goodness of sex will only make it more attractive, but our fear tactics that depict sex as dirty and dangerous only instill guilt and create confusion (as when musician Butch Hancock laments that growing up in Lubbock, Texas, taught him that "sex is the most awful, filthy thing on Earth, and you should save it for someone you love"). Our youth need the ability to trust, risk, and gladly defer certain joys because they have come to understand their sexual lives in terms of a bigger vision than their own personal pleasure or their own personal safety.

When our moral lives are shaped by fear, and safety is worshiped as the highest good, we are tempted to make health and security the primary justifications for right action. We thus lead timid lives, fearing the risks of bold gestures. Instead of being courageous, we are content to be safe. Instead of being hopeful, we make virtues of cynicism and irony, which in turn keep us a safe distance from risky commitments. We are more likely to tell our children to "be careful" than to "be good." The extravagant vision that would change the world gets traded in for the passive axiom "do no harm." Our moral lives atrophy on this new diet of self-protection.

A crucial part of the argument I want to make in this book is that many people do bad things not so much because they are evil, but because they are fearful. The relentless pursuit of safety leads to uncharitable hearts, for we fear letting go of the goods that might protect us against an uncertain future. In the name of security we refuse to love our enemies, because we assume that if we do not answer violence with violence, we will be forever victimized. Because we wish to be careful, we do not open our lives to strangers, fearing they will take advantage of our hospitality. It is fear that constricts our hearts and thus fear that makes Jesus's ethic of risky discipleship look crazy, unrealistic, and irresponsible. Yet the "virtues" of the ethic of safety—suspicion, preemption, and accumulation—turn out to be but "splendid vices" (St. Augustine's description of Roman "virtues").

Suspicion: "Don't Talk to Strangers"

My wife and I recently decided it was time to begin talking to our children about "strangers." We checked some books out of the library that dealt with the topic in fairly balanced ways, but the message was clear: "Don't talk to strangers." Of course, we want to protect our children, but we do not want to teach them to identify the stranger with danger. I recently saw an anti-crime billboard that read, "When you know all your neighbors, the bad guys stand out." This presumes, of course, that we equate the stranger, whoever is not "one of us," with "bad guys." This kind of undue suspicion is what we wish to avoid teaching our children. No, I don't want my children talking to strangers, but I *do* want them to learn that hospitality is a virtue and that welcoming the stranger is welcoming Christ himself.

Suspicion becomes a virtue in the culture of fear, because if we assume that we are always "at risk," we will always treat others as potential threats. Furedi tells of a "Stranger Danger" campaign that took place in Leeds,

England, in 1988.[13] Among the many messages that saturated the community was "One false move and you're dead." Looking at the effects on children of such "Stranger Danger" campaigns, one study concluded: "We have created a world for our children in which safety is promoted through fear. The message of campaigns such as 'One false move and you're dead' is one of deference to the source of the danger. That such a world can be advertised without apparent embarrassment by those responsible for the safety of children, and without provoking public outrage, is a measure of how far the unacceptable has become accepted."[14]

The mentality that turns suspicion into a virtue not only threatens family and community life but has become a dominant feature of the post-9/11 American political landscape. Beginning in January 2004 U.S. customs officers began photographing and fingerprinting all foreign visitors who entered the United States on a visa. While this may prove to be an effective security measure, it does heighten the perception that everyone entering from a nation that requires a visa is a suspect, treated the same way as police suspects who have mug shots and fingerprints taken upon arrival at the station. In an interview on NPR's *Weekend Edition,* news analyst Daniel Schorr reflected on the significance of these actions: "To me it suggests the kind of world we live in today, we are a besieged society; whether it be fingerprints, whether it be putting people in jail and leaving them there without trial . . . all of these things are in a sense, for any Al Qaeda out there, already a rather small advance to make, to make this society look so scared."[15] In many ways these new practices are just an extension of the identity checks already performed at customs. But what is troubling is the way they feed our self-perception as a society at risk. When we begin to do to foreign visitors the same things we do to suspected criminals, it is hard not to conclude that everyone coming in is, in fact, dangerous.

After the exodus from Egypt and their return to the Promised Land, the Israelites found themselves confronted by threatening strangers and dangerous enemies. Yet God commanded them, "When an alien resides with you in your land, you shall not oppress the alien. The alien who resides with you shall be to you as the citizen among you; you shall love the alien as yourself, for you were aliens in the land of Egypt: I am the Lord your God" (Lev. 19:33–34). We see Israel acting out this kind of welcome in the story of Ruth, where a Moabite woman is received, cared for, and gathered into the people of Israel.

This same pattern of hospitality plays an important role in the New Testament, where Jesus welcomes and shares meals with the "aliens" of his day—sinners and tax collectors, the sick and the outcast. Yet this is not an easy lesson to learn, and Jesus's disciples did not learn quickly. One day, on their way to Jerusalem, Jesus and his disciples entered a

Samaritan village where they were not well-received. James and John knew just what to do: "Lord, do you want us to command fire to come down from heaven and consume them?" (Luke 9:54). But Jesus rebuked them. There is a tension in the biblical story between God's calling to welcome the stranger, the outsider, even the enemy, and the countertendency to exclude and destroy those whose difference or diffidence is perceived as a threat. Suspicion can look very much like a virtue when people are afraid.

Preemption: "Do unto Others before They Do unto You"

The second "shadow virtue" of the ethic of safety is preemption. Preemption can take the form of fight or flight. As a kind of flight, preemption resembles Aquinas's notion of "contraction," making an anticipatory retreat from that which might harm us. In relationships, for instance, fear can cause us to flee from someone before they can flee from us. The high-school version of this involves breaking up with the other person before they can break up with you, but as we grow older this kind of preemptive mind-set can keep us from taking the risk of developing any meaningful and lasting relationships.

My wife and I recently attended a renewal-of-vows ceremony for some friends of ours. They had been married ten years, and the time seemed right to reenact and reaffirm their covenant. As the husband introduced the service, he admitted to the ways in which his own life had been far too determined by fear. He described the renewal of vows as "striking a blow against the empire of fear." Which, when I thought about it, made perfect sense. Marriage is an act that challenges all our fears of abandonment, rejection, and failure. To marry is to confront those fears and refuse to allow them to determine one's relationship. To renew vows in a culture of fear is to close the back door of preemptive flight and to throw oneself totally and precariously into the hands of another, and for Christians, to throw oneself and the other totally into the hands of God. Preemptive flight can prevent us from engaging life and love, from taking risks and accepting adventure. It is characterized by our own lost opportunities and possibilities.

When preemption combines with "fight" rather than "flight," we get the preemptive attack, which jeopardizes opportunities and possibilities of others. The connection of fear and violence is nothing new, but it is interesting to reflect on the cultural shift that has led some to justify violence not only in the face of an actual threat, but in the face of a potential threat. Though the "doctrine of preemption" was not created by George W. Bush, he was the first to name it as a determining principle in

U.S. foreign policy. In a formative speech delivered at West Point in the summer of 2002, Bush said, "Our security will require all Americans to be forward-looking and resolute, to be ready for preemptive action when necessary to defend our liberty and to defend our lives."[16] This vision was expanded into the *National Security Strategy* that Bush promulgated in September 2002. There he affirmed that "while the United States will constantly strive to enlist the support of the international community, we will not hesitate to act alone, if necessary, to exercise our right of self-defense by acting preemptively against such terrorists, to prevent them from doing harm against our people and our country."[17] Preemption meant that violence would be used before the threat had been actualized, that is, before there was reason to defend ourselves, before we were certain that we were in danger. The "Bush doctrine" expanded the justified use of violence exponentially, since strong suspicion alone could warrant a preemptive attack.

In the song "Devils & Dust," Bruce Springsteen imagines the plight of an American soldier enforcing a checkpoint in Iraq. This is, of course, an extremely dangerous job, especially since checkpoints have been a favorite target of suicide car bombers. The song does not aim to judge the soldier so much as lament what such constant fear will do to a good person's soul. Springsteen sings:

> I got my finger on the trigger
> But I don't know who to trust
> When I look into your eyes
> There's just devils and dust
>
> I got God on my side
> I'm just trying to survive
> What if what you do to survive
> Kills the things you love
> Fear's a powerful thing
> It can turn your heart black you can trust
> It'll take your God filled soul
> And fill it with devils and dust

By the end of the song Springsteen alters the refrain from "Fear's a powerful thing" to "Fear's a dangerous thing," reminding us that the fear inside of us may ironically become more dangerous than the threats outside of us.

The possibility that the violence we employ to calm our fears may actually "kill the things we love" became a tragic reality for one man on a London subway on July 22, 2005. The incident occurred during the tense weeks after terror attacks rocked London's transportation systems and just one day after a second set of bombs failed to detonate. Jean Charles de Menezes, a Brazilian electrician working in London, was being trailed by plainclothes police officers as he made his way to work. As he entered the Stockwell station the officers chased down de Menezes, brought him to the ground, and shot him multiple times in the head. Fearing he was a terrorist, the police had engaged the "shoot-to-kill protocol" recently implemented by Scotland Yard. This protocol defined certain circumstances in which officers were directed to shoot a suspect in the head without warning if they thought he might be ready to activate a bomb.[18] The man, as it turned out, was simply an electrician making his morning commute.

The London police and the British government referred to this incident as a tragic mistake, but the language of "mistake" hides the fact that this is precisely what we should expect from a strategy of preemption. It is the predictable "collateral damage" of a preemptive protocol. The very nature of preemption is to strike before the other person has struck. Only after the fact can one know whether the other person was planning to strike or not. In this case he was not. In the case of the Iraq war the lack of weapons of mass destruction reveals that Saddam Hussein was not prepared to strike either. Such misjudgments on a personal and a national scale are part and parcel of preemptive action. At de Menezes' funeral the Archbishop of Westminster, Cardinal Cormac Murphy-O'Connor, cut to the heart of the matter when he urged people not to "surrender to a logic of fear."[19] Such logic turns the killing of innocents into a "tragic necessity," lamentable but acceptable if it keeps us safe.

Accumulation: "Save for a Rainy Day"

Another way in which the ethic of safety distorts our perceptions is by tempting us to accumulate more and more wealth in order to stave off future misfortune. We fear losing our jobs. We fear that Social Security will not be there for us when we retire. We fear that our health-care benefits will not be sufficient to cover expensive treatments or long-term care in a nursing home. And so we come to believe that the more we have, the less we need to fear. We accumulate as an act of prudence, trying to secure ourselves against an uncertain future. And if there were no God, this would be exactly the right thing to do.

This is far different from greed, we tell ourselves. This accumulation of wealth can easily be described as wise financial planning. I've been told by a friend who is a financial planner that my wife and I will need over a million dollars to retire "comfortably." I don't really know what "comfortably" means to this person, but the very language of "comfort" suggests something far less than extravagance. Indeed, the very matter-of-factness of the statement carries a subtle threat that if we do not have such a grand sum tucked away, we will live *uncomfortably* in our older years. But what does all that pressure to hit the million mark do to our ability to be generous here and now?

In the Lord's Prayer, Jesus teaches his followers to pray, "Give us this day our daily bread" (Matt. 6:11). We would do well to note that Jesus does not encourage us to pray for tomorrow or the next day or for enough money to secure the whole month's grocery bill. Rather, he calls us to be content with God's provision for the day. Just a few verses later Jesus tells his followers, "Do not store up for yourselves treasures on earth" (Matt. 6:19). These teachings indicate that following Jesus will involve living in the insecurity of letting go of our "stored-up" goods, releasing them to those who have needs now so that we might be the means by which God gives to them their daily bread. Excessive fearfulness makes us incapable of welcoming such vulnerability and thereby incapable of welcoming the daily gift of God's provision.

With our moral lives so deformed by fear, how can we hope to reclaim our birthright as nonanxious recipients of God's gifts? It might seem that the best response would be to rid ourselves of fear entirely, to live as fearless people. But fearlessness, as I will show in the next chapter, is a temptation we need to resist.

Questions for Discussion

1. If our specific fears are largely learned, then how are they taught? Do we teach them consciously or unconsciously? Does this teaching come through family, school, culture, or all of the above? Do you have any particularly strong fears or phobias? Can you remember how you learned them?

2. Look back at the songs discussed in this chapter, "The Places You Have Come to Fear the Most," "This Ruined Puzzle," and "Devils & Dust." What stood out to you in the lyrics of these songs? Is there a word, phrase, or metaphor that you thought was particularly helpful or interesting? Can you think of any other songs that speak to the issue of fear in our lives?

3. Do you or those around you seem to live by an "ethic of safety"? Can you give any examples of how our culture makes safety a moral issue? Would you say that "safety" is the most important thing in your life? If not, what is it that you seek more than that?

4. Do you find yourself suspicious of other people as you go about your daily activities? What makes them seem suspicious—is it how they look? or what they are doing? Do you find that your level of suspicion has increased since 9/11?

5. In what ways do you see preemption at work in your life or in the lives of those around you? How can we avoid having a preemptive mind-set individually and as a culture?

6. How do you make judgments about accumulation in your life? Do you believe there is such a thing as accumulating too much? If so, how do you know when you've reached that point? Have you ever thought of your accumulation as a way of creating security in the future? Do you think that makes you less likely to share your wealth or your "stuff" with those in need?

3

Why Fearlessness Is a Bad Idea

■ The Brothers Grimm tell a peculiar tale of a boy who goes into the world to learn how to fear.[1] He is the younger of two sons and has little knowledge or skill, but he does have the odd trait of being unafraid of anything. When his father suggests that he learn something useful, he replies that he wishes to learn "how to shudder." So begins his journey to learn fear. What is most interesting about the story is that not only is the boy without fear, he is also without love or compassion. Indeed, he seems unable to relate to others in any way that is identifiably human. He throws an innocent man down the stairs of a church tower, leaves him lying crumpled in a corner, and goes home to bed. He beats an old man with an iron bar and seems utterly unmoved. The boy finally learns to shudder when his wife throws a bucket of cold water on him while he sleeps. He wakes up shouting out, "Oh, what is making me shudder? . . .Yes, now I know how to shudder." In the end it is not clear that he has really learned to fear so much as to be startled, but what is interesting about the story is the way it correlates lack of fear with lack of love. One might even suspect a causal relation—the boy lacks fear *because* he lacks love, since those who love nothing fear no loss.

While fearlessness might appear to be desirable on the surface, this folktale suggests it may be a disordered state, not a virtue but a vice. We fear evil because it threatens the things we love—family, friends, community, peace, and life itself. The only sure way to avoid fear, then, is to love less or not at all. If we loved nothing, we would have no fear, but this would hardly be considered a good thing. Perhaps this connection between fear and love helps explain the parenting fears I described above. Our love for our children grips us in a way that few loves do, and so our fear for them is greater in proportion to this great love.

So, contrary to those who speak simplistically of fear and love as opposites, we can see that they are related—fear is the shadow side of love. Our response to living in a dangerous world ought not to be an attempt at fearlessness but an attempt to feel fear in the right way, at the right time, and to the right extent. Again we can learn from Thomas Aquinas, who went so far as to say that "fear is born of love."[2] Because fear and love walk hand in hand, there is no way to eradicate one without losing the other. We would need to be concerned if we had no fear, for it would be a sign that we had no love. This helps explain why Aquinas calls fear a gift and fearlessness a vice.[3]

Fear and Love

Because fear is born of love, it can serve to awaken us to loves that have been neglected or taken for granted. In this way fear can be a gift. Fear exists in the nexus of love and limitation. We love much about our world, and yet our power to preserve what we love is limited. Indeed it is the very nature of our world to change. We participate in a web of life that includes both growth and decay, birth and death, victory and defeat. Limitation is part of what it means to live as mortals and to participate in a created world. Limitation and mortality are not evil but are part of what Swiss theologian Karl Barth called the "shadow side" of creation.[4] They are the shadows cast when the light of God's goodness shines upon a fragile and finite world. We might say that love in a changing world casts a shadow that hints at inevitable loss. The larger the love, the larger the shadow. The larger the shadow, the larger the fear. While some amount of fear is normal and natural, we must be careful not to allow the shadow of loss to diminish our ability to love and enjoy what is present. What is dangerous and destructive is not fear itself, but excessive fear.

St. Augustine, in his autobiography, *The Confessions,* reflects on the pain of love and loss as he remembers the death of a dear friend. His words give voice to feelings that are familiar to any who have lost those they love, whether to death, divorce, disease, or betrayal. He writes, "Black grief closed over my heart and wherever I looked I saw only death. . . . Everything I had shared with my friend turned into hideous anguish without him. My eyes sought him everywhere, but he was missing; I hated all things because they held him not, and could no more say to me, 'Look here

40

he comes!' as they had been wont to do in his lifetime when he had been away."[5] Like many who have faced loss, Augustine is tempted to reject love altogether, for every new love contains "the seeds of fresh sorrows."[6] Then Augustine turns to God and prays, "Turn us toward yourself, O God . . . for wheresoever a human soul turns, it can but cling to what brings sorrow unless it turns to you, cling though it may to beautiful things outside you and outside itself. Yet were these beautiful things not from you, none of them would be at all. They arise and sink; in their rising they begin to exist and grow toward their perfection, but once perfect they grow old and perish."[7] So Augustine comes to recognize that transience is built into the nature of a created world. Only God does not change; only God is by nature eternal.

Because love and loss are natural, so is fear. Fear is born of love, but it is also born of the knowledge that all loves are subject to decay, and death spares no one. To love is to plant seeds of sorrow. And yet, the recognition of our limitation can produce not only lament but also gratitude. For if fear is born of love, then fear can also awaken us to loves that we have taken for granted, overlooked, or forgotten. Sometimes it is when our loves are most threatened that we see them most clearly. Those who face near-death experiences or terminal illnesses often report that their love for family and friends is awakened and that their appreciation of everyday life is renewed. Columnist George Packer quotes a survivor of the 9/11 World Trade Center attacks as saying, "I like this state. I've never been more cognizant in my life."[8] Such a response to 9/11 may seem at first blush somewhat strange, but it should not surprise us. Fear alerts us to our loves in a powerful way. It can focus our actions and clarify our priorities. Aquinas observes that "if the fear be moderate, without much disturbance of the reason, it conduces to working well, in so far as it causes a certain solicitude, and makes a man take counsel and work with greater attention."[9] Moderate fear can imbue one's life and work with a sense of seriousness and import. Perhaps this is why St. Benedict, the sixth-century monk, lists among his "instruments of good works" the injunction to "keep death before one's eyes daily."[10]

I can almost imagine Benedict tapping his toes to the hugely popular country song "Live Like You Were Dyin'." Tim McGraw sings about a man in his forties who is diagnosed with a terminal illness that changes the way he lives. He finds that keeping death daily before his eyes helps him to keep life daily before his eyes. When asked what he did when he found out the news of his illness, the man in the song replies that he went sky-diving, mountain climbing, and bull riding, that he "loved deeper" and "spoke sweeter" and "gave forgiveness I'd been denyin'." Then he says, "some day I hope you get the chance / To live like you were dyin'."

Such transformations are not only the material of country songs. In *The Gift of Peace*, Joseph Cardinal Bernardin, the former Archbishop of Chicago, writes powerfully about the transformation in his life after he was diagnosed with terminal cancer. Though he does not go skydiving or bull riding, he does spend time in the community of cancer patients and others with serious illnesses, where he discovers that "those in this community see things differently. Life takes on new meaning, and suddenly it becomes easier to separate the essential from the peripheral."[11] In a pastoral letter Bernardin notes that through his struggle with cancer, "I came to realize how much of what consumes our daily life is trivial and insignificant."[12] This altered gaze, this truthful seeing, can be a gift that arises out of our limitation and is fed by moments when fear reminds us both of our loves and of our fragility. Apart from a sense of threat and fear, we are sometimes lulled into a false security that leads us to take our loves for granted and thus to cease to rejoice in them. Fear awakens us to our loves because in fear we imagine our loves lost.

So the one thing we do *not* have to fear is fear itself, for fear can and often does serve the good of life and love.

Fear of God

The biblical concept of "the fear of the Lord" also equates fear with gift. It is "the beginning of wisdom" according to Proverbs 1:7, and Isaiah 11:2 lists "the fear of the Lord" as a gift of the Spirit. Nonetheless, this phrase is widely misunderstood and can be used in ways that sound like anything but a gift. Biblical scholar Ellen Davis notes that upholding fear "as a healthy and necessary disposition toward God" represents for many modern readers "one of the most offensive things in the Old Testament."[13] One can understand why some people would take offense, given how appeals to the "fear of God" can be used to coerce and threaten.

For instance, the "Fear God" merchandise I mentioned in chapter 1 provides a wonderfully awful example of this theological mistake. The T-shirt logos presume that fearing God has everything to do with manipulating people through threats: "Jesus is coming back and this time no one is going to cross him—Fear God" and "Fine. Don't keep God's commandments. Just don't come crying to me when you end up flat on your face like Goliath—Fear God." Tragically, this appeal to coercive and threatening power is what many people think of when they hear "fear of the Lord." Fortunately, this is neither the only nor the best way to interpret the biblical phrase.

First of all, we have to try to reconcile "fear of the Lord" with the God of grace who calms our fears and delivers us from evil. We are often told in scripture *not* to fear precisely because God is with us: "God is our refuge and strength, a very present help in trouble. Therefore we will not fear" (Ps. 46:1–2). "Do not fear" is the message of Moses to the people of Israel (Deut. 31:6), of Isaiah to a destroyed Jerusalem (Isa. 40:9), of the angel Gabriel to Mary (Luke 1:30), of Jesus to Paul (Acts 18:9), and of Jesus to John on the island of Patmos (Rev. 1:17). We are told that "There is no fear in love, but perfect love casts out fear" (1 John 4:18). Why would we fear God if God is love, the source of our comfort and deliverance?

Yet at other times scripture suggests that the God who is love is the very one we should fear. Abraham is thus praised by the angel: "Now I know that you fear God" (Gen. 22:12), and over and again we read that "the fear of the Lord is the beginning of wisdom" (Job 28:28; Ps. 111:10, Prov. 1:7, Mic. 6:9). The words of Moses to the Israelites illustrate the paradox of fear in the Bible, "Do not be afraid; for God has come only to test you and to put the fear of him upon you so that you do not sin" (Exod. 20:20). Do not be afraid, he seems to say, because God has come to make you afraid. What is going on here? Does God calm our fears or make us fearful?

It would seem that God promises to calm our fears of worldly dangers, while at the same time urging us to fear God. Jesus echoes this twofold approach to fear when he tells his disciples, "Do not fear those who kill the body but cannot kill the soul; rather fear him who can destroy both soul and body in hell" (Matt. 10:28). One might mistakenly assume that Jesus is saying we should not fear lesser earthly fears precisely because we have a much bigger threat to worry about—God. But does it make any sense to speak of God as something that threatens the things we love? Are we meant to "fear" God in that way?

Ellen Davis notes that some Bible translators today render the phrase "fear of the Lord" as "reverence for the Lord." She agrees that "reverence is part of what the sages mean to commend to us," but she argues that this translation leaves too much out. "The writers are speaking first of all of our proper gut response to God," she writes. "Fear is the unmistakable feeling in our bodies, in our stomachs and our scalp, when we run up hard against the power of God. From a biblical perspective, there is nothing neurotic about fearing God. The neurotic thing is *not* to be afraid, or to be afraid of the wrong thing. That is why God chooses to be known to us, so that we may stop being afraid of the wrong thing. When God is fully revealed to us and we 'get it,' then we experience the conversion of our fear."[14] God wants to turn our fear away from worldly objects that only manipulate, control, and coerce us, and to redirect it to the God whose power does not threaten our true good but sustains it.

Describing our experience of God as "fear" makes a certain kind of sense, then, when understood rightly. To return to Davis, "The time comes in every life—and more than once—when we are personally confronted with the power that spread out the heavens like a sequined veil, that formed us out of dust and blew breath into our lungs, that led Israel through the Red Sea on dry land and left Pharaoh's whole army floating behind. If we can experience that power close up and *not* be gripped in our guts by the disparity between God and ourselves, then we are in a profound state of spiritual slumber, if not acute mental illness. 'Fear of the Lord' is the deeply sane recognition that we are not God."[15] Fear of the Lord, understood in this way, shares more in common with our sense of awe at something wondrously bigger than ourselves than it does with our anxiety in the face of an evil that seeks to harm us.

Aquinas also helps us untangle the ways "fear" can be applied to God by making a distinction between "servile fear" and "filial fear." Aquinas explains "servile fear" by drawing on the analogy of a servant who does right because he fears the punishment of the master. Though this kind of fear might encourage us to do good, it should not be considered a "gift" from God, since it is tied too closely to worldly power. Aquinas's description of "filial fear," on the other hand, draws on the analogy of a parent and a child, a relation that is much more like that between God and humankind. This fear is based in love and affection and presumes that we know God not as a threatening judge but as a loving father. Like a child who fears harming her relationship with her parents more than she fears being "grounded" for doing wrong, our fear of God has to do with a proper desire not to be separated from God. Because we love God, we fear anything that would harm our relationship with God. So, filial fear can turn us from bad choices, because we recognize that what could be lost is something we love greatly. Understood in this way, the "fear of God" is a gift of the Holy Spirit that can help us resist evil and pursue the good.

The Vice of Fearlessness

Fear, then, is the natural counterpart to love and can even be a gift if it is not excessive. This view of fear challenges a good deal of conventional wisdom and pop psychology. In one recent book, a self-help rabbi goes so far as to say that "you must first abandon all thoughts that fear serves a useful purpose in your life. . . . you must accept that fear is not only harmful but evil, not only unhelpful but deeply destructive. Fear has not a single healthy application in any area of life. Period."[16] On the surface this may sound wise, even inspiring. But in practice we need to ask, what is the price we would have to pay for fearlessness?

Aquinas argues that we can become fearless in three ways (and none of them is good): through a "lack of love" (loving nothing enough to fear its loss), through "dullness of understanding" (not knowing or acknowledging the danger or threat), or through "pride of soul" (refusing to believe that one is susceptible to loss).[17] In contemporary terms, we might think of these as "the security of detachment," "the bliss of ignorance," and "the pursuit of invulnerability."

Like the boy in the Grimm fable, one way to be without fear is through "the security of detachment," loving nothing enough to care if it is lost. After the death of his friend, Augustine was tempted to avoid love, to detach from the people and things of this world. I would imagine that most of us who have experienced significant pain or loss have felt tempted to seek refuge in this kind of fearlessness. Rather than live with the fear that we will be hurt once more, we build walls, resolving never to sow the seeds of sorrow again. We try to protect our hearts from pain, but in the process we shield ourselves from love. Our hearts are contracted, our relationships diminished. This posture of detachment, while it may temporarily calm our fear of loss, comes at too high a price.

Another way to become fearless is through the "the bliss of ignorance." This kind of fearlessness can arise through a passive denial of the real dangers that exist (perhaps this is the kind of fearlessness of someone who continues to smoke despite the proven dangers) or through a willful ignorance that amounts to a kind of recklessness. Our culture of fear has produced an interesting backlash, especially among the young, in which recklessness becomes an attractive form of rebellion. Of course, recklessness disguises itself as courage. But true courage does not lack fear altogether; it feels fear appropriately but does not allow fear to control one's life, to diminish one's loves, or to divert one's pursuit of the good. Recklessness as fearlessness produces a desire to create dangerous situations in order to experience and then overcome fear (one troubling example of this is the increasingly popular practice of intentional asphyxiation, often tied to erotic stimulation). A reckless fearlessness, however, does not really overcome fear so much as give in to an uncritical fascination with fear.

Of course, just as marketers have found ways to profit from fear, so they have found ways to profit from fearlessness. Merchandise with the "No Fear" logo has become hugely popular among the participants in extreme sports. These T-shirts and boardshorts wage a campaign of fearlessness. For the skydiver the logo reads, "At 200 feet no one can hear you scream: No Fear," and for surfers a shark image is superimposed on the words "Bite Me: No Fear." What is problematic here is not that people wish to engage in thrilling and exciting new sports, but that these sports get narrated, especially by the marketplace, as expressions of fearlessness rather than courage.

The final path of fearlessness, and perhaps the most dangerous, is "the pursuit of invulnerability." In his 2005 State of the Union address, George

W. Bush asserted that one of our responsibilities "to future generations is to leave them an America that is safe from danger, and protected by peace. We will pass along to our children all the freedoms we enjoy—and chief among them is freedom from fear."[18] The sentiment here cannot be disputed, for of course we wish for our children to be free from fear. And yet, we have to ask, what does it take to have no fear? The only way for government to assure a freedom from fear is to make its people invulnerable. Aside from whether or not that is even possible, what price would have to be paid in its pursuit?

The pride of soul that Aquinas talks about includes not only the "it can't happen to us" mentality that was once and for all shaken in the United States by the events of 9/11, but also the "it won't happen to us" mentality that pridefully supposes that an individual, community, or nation could become so powerful that it could not be threatened. How could we possibly assure freedom from fear unless we were able to destroy not only all imminent threats but also all potential threats? The price that we pay is waging "preemptive war," imprisoning suspicious individuals without charges or trial, and torturing prisoners to gain information. The question is what kind of person or nation one must become in order to pursue the illusion of invulnerability. Is it worth it?

We seek invulnerability because we fear the loss of what we love, but could it be that our attempts at invulnerability, whether on a national or a personal level, only destroy the things we wish to save? In a very interesting way the *Star Wars* epic tackles this very question. Now that the prequels have been completed, one can see more clearly that fear, fearlessness, evil, and invulnerability constitute the key themes in the story's unfolding drama.

Star Wars: A Parable of Fear

The six-episode saga of *Star Wars* focuses on the destiny of Anakin Skywalker, his torments, his fears, his turn to evil, and his final return to good. Over the course of writing and directing this ambitious modern myth, George Lucas wrestles profoundly with the roots of evil and sees clearly its connection to both fear and fearlessness.

In *Episode One—The Phantom Menace,* we meet young Anakin Skywalker, who is, along with his mother, a slave. Qui-Gon, a Jedi master, frees Anakin, believing that he has the gifts and calling to be a Jedi, but Anakin's mother, Shmi, must be left behind. Before Qui-Gon leaves, Shmi relates the story of Anakin's miraculous birth, "There was no father. I carried him, I gave birth, I raised him. I can't explain what happened."[19] With this clear allusion to the biblical story of the virgin birth, Lucas makes Anakin the Christ-figure of the story. But, unlike Jesus, who fended off temptation in the desert, Anakin's salvific work will come only after a long detour through evil. In a way, *Star Wars* could be interpreted as an extended reflection on what might have happened if Jesus had said yes to Satan's offer.

Qui-Gon wants to train Anakin to be a member of the Jedi, a diverse group of humans and other creatures who have a special connection to "the Force" (a kind of cosmic, spiritual energy). He believes that Anakin is "the chosen one," born to defeat the dark side and restore balance to the Force, but he must convince the Jedi Council. As the council begins to interview Anakin, Yoda (a froglike Jedi with unusual syntax) probes his fear:

Yoda: How feel you?

Anakin: Cold, sir.

Yoda: Afraid are you?

Anakin: No, sir.

Yoda: See through you we can.

Mace Windu: Be mindful of your feelings.

Ki-Adi-Mundi: Your thoughts dwell on your mother.

Anakin: I miss her.

Yoda: Afraid to lose her I think, hmm?

Anakin: What has that got to do with anything?

Yoda: Everything! Fear is the path to the Dark Side. Fear leads to anger. Anger leads to hate. Hate leads to suffering. I sense much fear in you.[20]

Yoda's words foreshadow the path that will lead Anakin to embrace evil and ultimately become Darth Vader. Nonetheless, many on the council believe Anakin to be the chosen one, spoken of by the prophets, and they allow him to train.

In *Episode II*, Anakin's fear becomes reality as his mother is kidnapped and killed by the sandpeople. Anakin is filled with rage, and he attacks their village, murdering not only the men but women and children as well. This scene augurs a later, even darker moment in *Episode III*, when Anakin will slay a gathering of children who are being trained as Jedis. As Yoda predicted, Anakin's fear has multiplied and born fruit in anger, hate, and suffering.

In defiance of the Jedi rule, Anakin secretly marries Padme Amidala, and just as he had premonitions of his mother's death, he begins to have premonitions of his wife's death. The fear of losing Padme provokes Anakin's turn to the dark side. Tempted by false promises, he seeks the power to

47

deliver Padme from death, to make her invulnerable. He boasts, "One day, I will become the greatest Jedi ever. I will even learn how to stop people from dying." Chancellor Palpatine (who turns out to be the Dark Lord Darth Sidious) tempts Anakin with the promise of such power. He recounts the legend of Darth Plagueis "the wise."

> Chancellor Palpatine: Darth Plagueis was a Dark Lord of the Sith, so powerful and so wise he could use the Force to influence the midi-chlorians to create life. . . . He had such a knowledge of the dark side that he could even keep the ones he cared about from dying.
>
> Anakin: He could actually save people from death?
>
> Chancellor Palpatine: The Dark Side of the Force is a pathway to many abilities some consider to be unnatural. . . .
>
> Anakin: Is it possible to learn this power?
>
> Chancellor Palpatine: Not from a Jedi.

Later Palpatine promises more explicitly, "Learn the Dark Side of the Force and you will save your wife from certain death." He implies that he can train Anakin to have such power, and the temptation to become invulnerable and thus overcome his fear of Padme's loss proves too much for Anakin. He joins forces with the Dark Lord, all the while trying to convince himself and Padme that he is doing the right thing. In the end Anakin's turn to the Dark Side ironically becomes the cause of Padme's death.

As the story unfolds it becomes clear that the Jedi fighters, though they recognize the connection between fear and evil, seek not so much to embody courage as to achieve a type of fearlessness: the security of detachment. This comes out clearly in the almost monastic Jedi prohibition of marriage, but it goes further to encourage a deeper detachment from all worldly things. Thus, Anakin's love for, attachment to, and eventual marriage to Padme become a hindrance to his training and his ultimate downfall. If he did not love so much, say his Jedi masters, he would not have been so tempted by the false security of the Dark Side.

We see this philosophy of detachment at work in Anakin's conversation with Yoda in *Episode III*:

> Yoda: Premonitions, premonitions. Hmm, these visions you have . . .
>
> Anakin: They are of pain, suffering, death . . .
>
> Yoda: Yourself you speak of, or someone you know?
>
> Anakin: Someone . . .
>
> Yoda: Close to you?
>
> Anakin: Yes.

Yoda: Careful you must be when sensing the future, Anakin. The fear of loss is a path to the Dark Side.

Anakin: I won't let these visions come true, Master Yoda.

Yoda: Death is a natural part of life. Rejoice for those around you who transform into the Force. Mourn them, do not. Miss them, do not. Attachment leads to jealousy. The shadow of greed, that is.

Anakin: What must I do, Master Yoda?

Yoda: Train yourself to let go of everything you fear to lose.

The Jedi way takes as a virtue what Aquinas would identify as a vice: the "lack of love" that attempts to overcome fear through detachment. Interestingly, though detachment is the Jedi way, the film suggests a critique of this position. At the end of *Episode III,* when Anakin has given himself to the instruction of Darth Sidious and has been transformed into Darth Vader, Yoda instructs Obi-Wan, the Jedi who trained Anakin, to find him and kill him. When Obi-Wan balks at the idea of killing his apprentice (apparently too attached he is), Yoda tells him: "Twisted by the Dark Side, young Skywalker has become. The boy you trained, gone he is. . . . Consumed by Darth Vader." Yoda's detachment frees him from any sentimental ties to the Anakin who is now "gone." But Obi-Wan, himself a bit of a rebel among the Jedi, refuses to believe that Anakin is lost for good. In the end, of course, Obi-Wan's reservations prove well founded. It is not true that "gone he is," consumed by darkness, for something of Anakin remains in Vader, a glimmer of good that will reappear. In the final episode, Anakin/Vader is revealed as the chosen one and fulfills the prophecy by killing Darth Sidious and returning balance to the Force. Had Obi-Wan followed Yoda's counsel, the consequences would have been disastrous. Thus, despite the positive portrayal of the Jedi in the films, the storyline itself questions the Jedi virtue of detachment precisely insofar as it could lead Yoda to pronounce a death sentence upon Anakin. In contrast to Yoda's detachment, Padme loves Anakin and thereby sees him more truly. She tells Obi-Wan on her death bed: "There is good in him. I know there is . . . still." At the end of *Episode VI* we see the redemption of Anakin/Vader, and we discover the truth in Padme's words.

The *Star Wars* saga serves as a kind of parable about fear and its consequences. In between epic battles, ewoks, droids, and Jar-Jar, the real story has to do with fear, what it can do to us, and how we can overcome it. The story teaches us that evil is not just the object of fear but it is the temptation that arises from fear. It is the temptation, as Bono put it, to "become a monster / So the monster will not break you."[21] Anakin becomes the monster of Darth Vader, but in the end the monster breaks him anyway. Padme dies and, in a way, Anakin dies too. The story teaches us that our response to fear cannot be fearlessness, either that of detachment or of invulnerability. Fearlessness is a bad substitute for courage.

In a culture of fear, this kind of film can be instructive if we take time to discover the themes that weave their way beneath the special effects. Yet the question remains, if fearlessness is not the answer, how do we respond rightly to the culture of fear? Can we put the genie back in the bottle, can we learn again to be reflective about fear, to reinscribe fear in a larger vision of life in which fear has a place but also can be kept in its place? This will be the work of the next chapter.

Questions for Discussion

1. What do you think of the Brothers Grimm story? Do you see a connection between fear and love in your own life?
2. What do you think about the idea that fear can be a gift? Have you (or someone you know) ever had an experience of fear that awakened you to your loves? Think about the World Trade Center survivor who said, "I like this state. I've never been more cognizant in my life." Do you remember having a sense of clarity or purpose after 9/11 that arose alongside the sense of fear?
3. If every new love contains the "seeds of fresh sorrows," then why do we love at all? Why not just avoid love, avoid loss, and avoid fear?
4. How have you traditionally understood the biblical phrase "fear of God"? How do you think non-Christians in the culture hear that phrase? Did reading this chapter change the way you think about fear of God? Do you think fearing God can be a gift?
5. Fearlessness is a problem not just because it robs us of the gifts fear can bring, but also because of the price we pay to be fearless. Do you find yourself more tempted to avoid fear through "the security of detachment," "the bliss of ignorance," or "the pursuit of invulnerability"?
6. Discuss the role of fear and fearlessness in *Star Wars*. Having "become the monster" of Darth Vader, what does it take to turn Anakin back to the good in the final episode? Can you think of other films that deal with these issues?

Putting Fear in Its Place

■ During the 2004 presidential campaign, an editorial appeared in *USA Today* that depicted a life tragically overwhelmed by fear. The author described herself as a "security mom," representing the newest fashionable mom-bloc of voters (alongside "soccer moms" and "fast-food moms"). She writes,

> I am what this year's election pollsters call a "security mom." I'm married with two young children. I own a gun. And I vote. . . . The Sept. 11, 2001 terrorist attacks shook me out of my Generation X stupor. Unlike Hollywood and *The New York Times* and the ivory tower, I have not settled back casually into a Sept. 10 way of life. I have studied the faces on the FBI's most-wanted-terrorists list. When I ride the train, I watch for suspicious packages in empty seats. When I am on the highways, I pay attention to large trucks and tankers. I make my husband take his cellphone with him everywhere—even on a quick milk run or on a walk to the community pool. We have educated our 4-year-old daughter about Osama bin Laden and Saddam Hussein. She knows that there are bad men in the world trying to kill Americans everywhere. . . . [A]t night, we ask God to bless our troops as they risk their lives trying to kill the bad men before they kill us.[1]

As the father of three young boys, I can hardly imagine the words "kill them before they kill us" becoming part of our bedtime prayers. However, I am not surprised that someone so clearly racked with fear would feel a moral obligation to pass that fear on to her children. For her, it seems,

51

one's level of fear correlates with one's level of moral seriousness. In other words, she displays her political and social responsibility precisely by indulging in a fear-drenched response to 9/11. But if our level of fear shows our level of concern, how do we learn to say "enough" to fear? How much fear is enough to honor the lives lost on 9/11? How much fear is enough to ensure "never again"?

These, of course, turn out to be the wrong questions, for they give fear far too much power as a barometer of seriousness or outrage or sorrow. The baldness of such fear, its nakedness, its disconnection from any process of reflection, examination, and testing make it problematic at best and, at worst, morally dangerous, especially when we consider what it does to children to raise them on such a steady diet of dread.

So how do we begin the necessary examination and testing of fear? We need to understand fear better, to reconstruct our attitudes toward fear, and to find tools that will help us determine when fear is a natural and normal warning sign and when it is a toxic emotion that threatens our character and our communities. Fear itself is not evil, but it can become such. Excessive or disordered fear can drain the joy out of life, can constrict our vision and feed our hatreds. Fear can cause us to love less because we fear too much the seeds of sorrow that inhabit every love. Excessive fear can rob our lives of playfulness, exploration, and adventure. Fear can be a gift, but it can also be a poison. So, how do we know the difference? How do we put fear in its place?

As part of the bedtime routine in our house each night, we let our boys choose a song for us to sing. The hymn "Amazing Grace" tops the list of most requested songs (I suspect this is because it has so many verses and thus allows them to put off that final "good night" a bit longer). As I sang it to our boys the other night, I was struck by the words, "'Twas grace that taught my heart to fear / And grace my fears relieved." Well, I thought, which is it? Are we taught to fear or are we relieved of fear? As I thought further I realized the answer could be both. The hymn rightly suggests we need to be *taught* to fear, or better put, we need to be taught to fear well. But this teaching of fear, according to the hymn, must come by grace, for only grace can give us the courage to fear as we should. And grace goes on in the hymn, paradoxically, to relieve our fears even as it teaches them, which is to say, I think, that grace makes sure that our fears will not rule us. Grace puts fear in its place.

Fearing *What* We Should Not

Here again the wisdom of Thomas Aquinas will be helpful as we seek to map the terrain of fear. Aquinas observes that fear arises from the imagi-

52

nation of a future evil (something that threatens the loss of something we love) that is both imminent and hard to resist.[2] It follows, then, that fear can be disordered in two basic ways.[3] We can fear *what* we should not, either because the threat is not in fact great or imminent or because what we fear losing is not in fact a proper love (like riches or power). Or we can fear *as* we should not; that is, we may fear a real and legitimate threat but fear it excessively. Using Aquinas's definition, we can come up with a way of testing fear, so that we might become more reflective and less captive.

There are a number of ways that we might come to fear *what* we should not. If, as Aquinas tells us, the thing we fear is a future evil that is imminent, of great magnitude, and threatens a loss of something we rightly love, then fearing what we should not would be to fear an object that does not in fact include all of these characteristics. In other words, we might wrongly fear (a) an evil object that is imminent (present or fast-approaching) but not of great magnitude, that is, not so very big after all, and thus easily repelled; (b) an evil object that is of great magnitude but is not imminent and thus is not a present threat; (c) an evil object that is of great magnitude and imminent but is not really a threat after all; or (d) an evil object that is imminent, of great magnitude, and threatens something that we love but which we really should not (e.g., wealth or fame, in which case the object turns out not to be evil because it does not threaten a proper love). When we use Aquinas's definition as a benchmark, as a way of becoming more reflective about our fear, then we are on our way to putting fear in its place.

So let us examine these criteria more closely. First, we might fear something that is imminent but not of great magnitude. This is the stuff of phobias: fear of spiders, heights, crowds, or small places. Phobias involve fearing excessively something that is part of everyday life but which is not actually of great magnitude, that is, does not pose a significant threat.

Second, we might fear an evil object that is of great magnitude but is not in fact an imminent threat, such as shark attacks or lightning strikes. Aquinas writes, "Since fear arises *from the imagination of future evil,* . . . whatever removes the imagination of the future evil removes fear also. Now it may happen . . . that an evil may not appear as about to be . . . through being remote and far off: for, on account of the distance, such a thing is considered as though it were not to be. Hence we either do not fear it, or fear it but little."[4] So, one way to test our fear is to ask whether the evil we fear is far off or close at hand. For if an evil is "remote and far off," we should fear it either not at all or very little.

This insight is particularly important in our global village, where even evils that are very far off find their way to our front doorsteps through the newspaper and into our living rooms through television. Twenty-four-hour news stations make sure that disasters, assaults, kidnappings, and murders that once would have been known about only locally are now beamed nationally in minutes; and if the evil is particularly shocking, the news spreads quickly around the world. In this way our imaginations bring everything close. They bring close evils that are in fact far away, thus making us fear when in fact we should not.

Gerbner's "mean world syndrome" suggests something similar happens with fictional television. He argues that "if you are growing up in a home where there is more than, say, three hours of television per day, for all practical purposes you live in a meaner world—and act accordingly—than your next-door neighbor who lives in the same world but watches less television. The programming reinforces the worst fears and apprehensions and paranoia of a people."[5] How easy it is for us to misjudge the imminence of danger, since via the television dangers of all sorts enter our homes nightly.

The failure to judge accurately the imminence of a threat also seems to be related to the magnitude of the threat. If the magnitude of an evil object is great, as is the case with terrorism or weapons of mass destruction, we easily lose perspective as we attempt to judge its imminence. Thus, because of the magnitude of the evil we are tempted to fear it even if it is remote. Indeed, we are tempted to cease altogether making a distinction between evil that is close at hand and evil that is far away. This seems to be part of what is behind George W. Bush's doctrine of preemption and the U.S. invasion of Iraq.

Ron Suskind, a Pulitzer Prize-winning reporter, has traced the significance of what he calls the "Cheney Doctrine" on Bush's preemptive strategies. In response to a concern about Pakistan soon after 9/11, Cheney reportedly said, "If there's a 1 percent chance that Pakistani scientists are helping al Qaeda build or develop a nuclear weapon, we have to treat it as a certainty in terms of our response."[6] This became "a standard of action that would frame events and responses from the administration for years to come."[7] The U.S. response to any threat would be based on equating a 1 percent chance with absolute certainty. The magnitude of the possible evil was so large that imminence, probability, evidence of actual danger, no longer seemed to matter.

Many of us, government and people alike, are no longer sure what difference it makes if an evil is near at hand or far away, because all evils have been brought near, because of their sheer magnitude, because of political decision, or because of media exposure. Even evils that are "far off" (either in terms of literal distance or in terms of their likelihood) must be attacked as though they were near. We have become either incapable or unwilling to make what was, to Aquinas, a fundamental distinction that would help us fear well by fearing less.

54

A third way in which we might fear what we should not is to fear an object that may be of magnitude and imminent but does not actually threaten a loss of what we love. Perhaps we see this in the ways that fear has entered the political debate over gay unions. The question of gay unions is certainly one of magnitude, if by that we mean something that could produce far-reaching changes. It is also imminent, in that many states are currently wrestling with the issue of gay unions, and almost every church body is enmeshed in controversies surrounding homosexuality. The question, however, is whether gay unions are properly a cause of fear. That is, even if one believes that the church cannot support gay unions, do we need to be *afraid* of such unions or of homosexuals themselves?

Those who describe their opposition to gay unions as a "defense of marriage" seem to imply that allowing these unions will threaten the loss of something we properly love, marriage, and thus that gay unions are something to be feared. But is there any evidence that allowing gay unions will make heterosexual marriages less stable? Indeed, such a claim seems counterintuitive, since it suggests that gay people who wish to enter publicly into faithful lifelong covenants are in fact a threat to faithful lifelong covenants. Could it even happen that visible, faithful gay unions lived with integrity and love would spur on heterosexual marriages to greater faithfulness? There appears to be no logical reason to assume that allowing gay unions will threaten traditional marriage. This is not to say that gay unions should therefore be blessed by the church, only that fear does not help us make a judgment about this. We can and do at times fear the wrong things (for instance, not long ago many feared the consequences of interracial marriage). Thus, to invoke fear first, as if an appeal to fear is the same thing as a moral argument, is to circumvent much-needed conversation and discernment.

A third way in which we might fear what we should not is to fear an evil object that does, in fact, threaten something we love, but something that we *should not* love. Aquinas calls this "worldly fear," since it is based on "worldly love," that is, "the love whereby a man trusts in the world as his end."[8] This kind of fear turns us from God, since our fear of losing worldly loves makes us cling more tightly and attend more closely to them. When we love money, power, possessions, fame, leisure, or status, we fear their loss, and when we fear their loss we focus more energy on their preservation. Though we often imagine that the accumulation of worldly goods makes us more secure, Aquinas points out that such accumulation tends to make us more afraid, since the more we have, the more we have to lose. He notes that "inordinate fear is included in every sin; thus the covetous man fears the loss of money, the intemperate man the loss of pleasure, and so on."[9] Thus, the wealthy and powerful, who have the most resources to fend off impending evils, are rarely less fearful and often more so than those who have less (think of the layers of defense that surround the wealthy and the powerful: bodyguards, security guards, fences, and alarm systems).

I have noticed this correlation of fear and affluence in my own life. I used to drive a twenty-year-old Chevy Nova. I never locked the doors. But as the family grew, we traded in the Nova for a relatively new minivan. Then I began locking the doors. Now I have something to lose, and now I have something to fear. It's only natural, isn't it, that when you have "good stuff" you fear its loss more than when you have "bad stuff" (or no stuff). One way of testing whether our possessions have begun to possess us would be to reflect on the fear we have of losing them. When we have a high level of fear at the thought of losing our stuff, it is likely an indication that we are holding our "stuff" too tightly, refusing the open hand of generosity, thinking of ourselves as owners of our property rather than as stewards of God's property. Much of the fear-mongering described in the above chapters relies on our loving what we should not, on our caring more than we should about money, pleasure, and status. So marketers, politicians, and media executives not only prey on our disordered desires, but seek *to instill* such desires. If we can no longer control our love of worldly goods and pleasures, then we are easy prey for marketers who will gladly take advantage of our compulsions and addictions.

Fearing *as* We Should Not

Fear can become distorted or, to use Aquinas's term, "disordered," not just when we fear *what* we should not but when we fear *as* we should not; that is, when we fear *excessively.* In this case we may well fear things worth fearing, like divorce and heart disease, both of which are statistically common, or death itself, which is certain. But if we fear divorce, heart disease, or even death excessively, then we no longer fear rightly.

So, how do we know when fear is excessive? According to Aquinas, "reason dictates that certain goods are to be sought after more than certain evils are to be avoided. Accordingly when the appetite shuns what the reason dictates that we should endure rather than forfeit others that we should rather seek for, fear is inordinate and sinful."[10] Aquinas gets a bit complicated here, but what he is saying is simply that we fear excessively when we allow the avoidance of evil to trump the pursuit of the good. When we fear excessively we live in a mode of reacting to and plotting against evil rather than actively seeking and doing what is good and right. Excessive fear causes our scope of vision to narrow, when what is needed is for it to be enlarged.

When we are thinking about the fear of losing material things, it is good to remember that the real goal is to avoid fearing *excessively*, for it is not always wrong to fear the loss of our possessions. This is true for two reasons. First, says Aquinas, losses of money or power make us feel that we have fewer defenses against other threats to our deeper loves. Aquinas asks the question "whether defect is the cause of fear." By "defect" he means a lack of something like wealth, power, strength, or friends. He answers that these defects *can* be a cause of fear, because what we fear ultimately are those evils that are not easily repelled, and "it is owing to some lack of power that one is unable easily to repulse a threatening evil."[11] In this sense, then, defect, or lack, is a kind of second-level fear, a fear not directly of the evil object but a fear that one will not have the resources to stave off the threat. So, according to Aquinas, we are not wrong to fear the level of "defect" that would make us vulnerable to future evil. For instance, we rightly fear the kind of poverty that would lead to malnourishment or ill health for our children. This is not a sign of an inordinate lust for worldly goods but a proper desire to have what we need to care for those we love.

Second, Aquinas turns to Augustine to remind us that although "temporal things are goods of the least account,"[12] they are nonetheless "goods." He continues, "Hence their contraries are indeed to be feared; but not so much that one ought for their sake to renounce that which is good according to virtue."[13] That is, we must not seek to protect our possessions at the expense of doing what is good and right. So, for instance, it is not wrong to fear the loss of one's home, but it is wrong to fear the loss of one's home so much that one limits hospitality in order to secure one's household. We might ask, then, whether gated communities do not represent a kind of disordered love in which the desire to protect the lesser good of one's property leads a person to reject the greater good of hospitality.

The connection between affluence and fear has been driven home for me in my contact with some fellow Christians from Uganda. My church sponsors a ministry to the pygmies in Uganda. The pygmy tribes used to live in the Bwindi Impenetrable Forest, but logging and poaching led to environmental legislation that made development and habitation in the rain forest illegal, even for the pygmies. Since the 1990s the pygmies have become refugees. To further complicate matters, they were traditionally nomadic, wandering through the rain forest, settling only for short periods of time before moving on. Now that they have been forced out of the forest, they must not only find land, but learn the skills of living in permanent settlements. In Uganda they are the least of the least. The priests who run the mission visit the United States regularly, and we periodically send teams to them. What is most remarkable to those of us who assist in this ministry is the deep joy displayed by the Ugandans with whom we have contact. Despite living in a region that suffers from high mortality rates and the ever present danger of disease, starvation, and civil unrest, these Ugandans could not be rightly described as living in fear.

One evening, as a group of us from the church reflected on the remarkable peacefulness and good-naturedness of our Ugandan friends, we began to wonder whether their expectations of life were so much lower that they were not anxious about what might happen to them next. But we decided it was truer to say that they simply refused to *have* expectations about what life owed them. The Ugandan priests in charge of the mission never voice frustration about the lack of sponsorships for the schoolchildren, even though the cost of food, school, and medical care for a month is less than many of us spend at Starbucks. They are somehow able to be grateful for every offering without being offended or angry that there is not more. Everything that comes their way is a gift from God; they are not burdened by a sense of entitlement. God does not owe them something, and even in the midst of devastating circumstances, they find reason to give God thanks.

We must be careful not to romanticize poverty, hunger, or sickness; nevertheless, there is among these Ugandan Christians and the pygmies a capacity for joy and thankfulness, a resistance to resentment, and an absence of fear that continually impress us and challenge us to look back at our own lives with a new perspective. When we have more, we have more to lose. When we have more to lose, we have more to fear. The attitude of entitlement saps us of our ability to give thanks, to receive the goods of life as gifts. When we feel entitled to what we have, we resent any threat to our possessions, yet when we fear losing the objects of our misplaced desire, we really fear God working in our lives.

As noted in chapter 3, having excessive fear tends to make us attack or contract. Thus, one way of testing whether our fear is excessive is to ask to what extent we have begun to turn in on ourselves or lash out at others. Has our fearful aggression caused us to ignore or interpret away Jesus's call to love the enemy? Has our contraction begun to stifle our joy? Has our commitment to self-preservation caused us to turn our backs on those who need us?

Fear is related to love in that when we love we fear the loss of that love. Joy is also related to love in that it is experienced in the presence of the beloved or when good comes to the beloved.[14] Thus, in relation to love, fear and joy become in a sense "second cousins." But when fear becomes disordered it relates to joy not as a relative but as an enemy. It casts a shadow over the presence of the beloved, as the possibility of future danger elbows aside present happiness. We find ourselves unable to rejoice in the presence of what we love, because we are too afraid of losing it.

One day a lawyer approached Jesus and asked him, "What must I do to inherit eternal life?" Jesus responds by reaffirming the Jewish teaching that we should love God and neighbor. The lawyer (being a lawyer) then asks for further clarification. "Who is my neighbor?" he asks. He asks a question of contraction, a question of limits. Where does my responsibility end? Perhaps it is even a question of fear. Remember, the lawyer wants to know how to inherit eternal life. Perhaps he fears eternal death. And if the circle of love is too wide, it becomes all the more difficult to keep the command. Jesus's response is to tell the story of the good Samaritan in which a man, beaten and robbed, is left by the side of the road. A priest and a Levite pass by but refuse to bother themselves with the hurting man. A Samaritan, however, passes by and willingly extends himself to the stranger, giving assistance, time, and money. "Which of these three, do you think, was a neighbor to the man who fell into the hands of the robbers?" Jesus asks. "The one who showed mercy," replies the lawyer. "Go and do likewise," says Jesus (Luke 10:25–37). Jesus refuses to confine our care and concern to a limited group. "Neighbor" is not a quality someone has to have in order to be cared for; rather, "neighbor" is a quality of those who show mercy to the broken. Such an extension of the heart cannot be achieved in a state of systolic fear, for we may find, as the Samaritan did, that the person in need is the very enemy we have been warned about.

Faith's Daring

Fifty years ago Hans Urs von Balthasar wrote words that still ring true today: "Only a Christian who does not allow himself to be infected by modern humanity's neurotic anxiety . . . has any hope of exercising a Christian influence on this age. He will not haughtily turn away from the anxiety of his fellow men and fellow Christians but will show them how to extricate themselves from their fruitless withdrawal into themselves and will point out the paths by which they can step out into the open, into faith's daring."[15] Faith must be daring, because following Jesus is risky. "Take up your cross and follow me," Jesus tells us, and "those who lose their life for my sake will find it." The call of discipleship does not promise security; rather, in the words of Dietrich Bonhoeffer, a German theologian and martyr under Hitler, "When Christ calls a man, he bids him come and die."[16]

I used to think that the angels in the Bible began their messages with "Do not be afraid" because their appearance was so frightening. But I have come to think differently. I suspect that they begin this way because the quieting of fear is required in order to hear and do what God asks of us. Fear makes it difficult to embrace the vulnerability involved in discipleship;

it tempts us to replace Jesus's ethic of risk with an ethic of security. In the end, following Jesus requires that we step out "into faith's daring."

Irish theologian David Ford writes about the ways our lives are shaped by "overwhelmings."[17] Some of these are good, and some are bad. It may be helpful to think about excessive fear as a kind of negative overwhelming. Ford notes that when dealing with overwhelming experiences, tinkering with small details is not so helpful—for instance, dealing with our fear of terrorism by storing a bin of canned food and duct tape in the basement.[18] Nor is it helpful to simply tell ourselves, "I should not be overwhelmed by this." We cannot command ourselves to feel less fear. Quite the contrary, our overwhelming fears need, themselves, to be overwhelmed by bigger and better things, by a sense of adventure and fullness of life that comes from locating our fears and vulnerabilities within a larger story that is ultimately hopeful and not tragic. Ford writes, "[Jesus] taught his disciples that there was no following the way of the kingdom of God without being willing to stake their life on it. . . . It is a basic instance of overwhelming: Abundance of life and immersion in death are inseparable. How can we hope to shape our lives wisely if we have not faced up to death and are willing to risk it?"[19] Only by facing death, our most primal fear, can we move ahead to embrace life with the great "nevertheless" that is God's gracious word to a broken world.

Putting Fear in Its Place: Diagnostic Questions

So, how do we put fear in its place? It could be helpful at this point to gather up some questions from this chapter that a person or a community could ask in a situation of fear. This is not a comprehensive list, but a starting place for reflection.

- Is the thing you fear actually present or fast-approaching? Or is it far off, either in terms of distance (like a tornado that is a hundred miles away), time (like something that won't likely happen for years), or likelihood (like something that happens to one out of a million people)?
- Is the thing you fear really powerful and able to cause you harm? Or is it something that is generally small and harmless?
- Is the thing you fear really a threat? That is, will it really cause you to lose something you love, or does it just seem scary because it is strange?
- Are you afraid of losing something that is of real importance? Or is that "something" a thing that you shouldn't be so concerned about in the first place?

- Do you fear so much that you are closing in on yourself or unjustly lashing out at others?
- Does your fear keep you from doing things you know you should do?
- Does your fear take away the joy you feel in the presence of things you love (like your family) because you are afraid of losing them?
- Is your fear the result of someone's attempt to manipulate you? Is anyone profiting from your fearfulness (like a business getting your money, a politician getting your vote, or a religious leader getting your offering)?

At this point, I'm tempted to say something like, "If you answered yes to any of these questions, please call the number on your screen." But this is not a screen, and I'm not giving you my number (yeah, you guessed it, I'm afraid of what you might do with it). Rather than leading to a free thirty-day trial of a quick solution to fear, these questions, preferably answered and discussed with others, are intended to begin a process (perhaps a long one) of putting fear in its place. They are intended to help us become reflective about fear rather than just being reactive to it.

Security Mom, Take Two

What then might we say to our "security mom"? It would be an achievement simply to convince her that the objects of her fear are not simply given, but are taught. We might help her become reflective about fear, to name its roots, to gain a vocabulary by which she could make judgments about proper and improper fears. This, in turn, might allow her to assess more clearly the real risks in her life—is it more likely that she is going to be a victim of terrorism or die in a car crash, and how should the answer to this impact her life? Perhaps we could help her distinguish between magnitude and imminence, noting that while the 2001 terrorist attacks were of great magnitude, such attacks are not in fact likely to happen to her. We might encourage her to reflect on whether her avoidance of unlikely evils leads her to neglect the giving and receiving of goods.

Beyond that we might invite her into an explicitly theological conversation, which is where our next chapters will take us. We could begin by talking about the church as a place where people come to share our fears in common and thus find courage together. We might talk about the real source of security being not in human strength but in divine providence. This would lead into a bigger and longer conversation about life's proper loves and humankind's proper end. In the mean time, the invitation to become reflective and critical about our fears might help her (and her daughter) avoid a life of contraction and thus become open to the vulnerable gifts that are received only by the open hand.

Questions for Discussion

1. What would you say to the security mom?
2. Try this test. First, think about how much you fear losing your house, your car, your savings account, or your job. Then, think about how much you fear being unloving, inhospitable, selfish, or impatient. Which do you fear more? Why?
3. Do you think the presence of frightening stories in the media (especially news and dramas) makes it difficult to weigh the imminence of a threat? Do you find that watching more TV makes you more afraid?
4. Think about some fear in your life, and then work through the diagnostic questions above. In what way do the questions help you "put fear in its place"? Which questions are most helpful? Are there any questions you think should be added to the list?
5. How do *you* interpret the words from "Amazing Grace": "'Twas grace that taught my heart to fear / And grace my fears relieved"?
6. This chapter discusses the parable of the Good Samaritan in relation to fear and contraction. Read the parable in Luke 10:25–37 and discuss your insights.

5

Community and Courage

■ If you have ever been home alone at night when you are used to having others in the house, you will know the experience of suddenly hearing noises—squeaks and thumps—that you had never noticed before. The empty house feels more threatening even if there is no real reason to believe you are in danger. Simply being alone can make us feel vulnerable. Being alone can make it difficult to put danger and fear in perspective. Without the presence of others to balance our perspectives, to strengthen our resolve, and to share our risks, living courageously can feel like a daunting task.

Loneliness and Fear

The epidemic of loneliness and alienation in our culture adds to our fear, since our own resources often seem a meager stay against outside threats. As Furedi notes, "Many people are literally on their own. Such social isolation enhances the sense of insecurity. Many of society's characteristic obsessions—with health, safety and security—are the products of this experience of social isolation."[1] Our culture of fear is also a culture of disconnection, and the two are often related.

Reality TV has presented us in recent years with particularly salient examples of isolation within artificial community. Shows such as *The*

Apprentice, The Bachelor, and *Survivor* set a group of contestants in a context of communal living and shared projects but in which the participants can work together only insofar as it helps each individual eventually defeat all the others. Thus, even as the contestants weep, rage, and bare their souls together, each contestant lives in fear that they will be the next one sent home. Such shows reveal the kinds of anxiety produced by a culture that highly prizes individual achievement even as we yearn for communal connection.

Though many today speak of the virtues of community, the practical realities of our lives make the experience of real community uncommon. We are more mobile than ever, which means many of us live far from a network of extended family. We participate in a competitive economy where the coworker is also the competition for that next promotion. In many families today both parents work, which means that even the bonds of the nuclear family can be strained as the two ships pass in the night. In addition, we live in a cultural context in which traditions, narratives, and communities have largely lost their moral authority. We imagine that our decisions should not be influenced by any source outside ourselves, and so we increasingly cannot distinguish judgments from preferences. When we cannot assume a shared social or moral vision, our sense of isolation grows.

Furedi sees a connection between our obsession with individual freedom and our isolation: "Whether they like it or not, people have been 'freed' from many of the relations which linked individuals together in the past, so, in principle, people are free to choose their lifestyles and relations. But in the absence of new forms of social solidarities, such freedom helps to intensify the sense of estrangement and of powerlessness. It is as if people must 'choose,' whether they like it or not. There was a time when a life which consisted of this kind of choosing was just called survival. The tendency to endow estrangement with the positive quality of lifestyle choice represents an attempt at reconciliation with powerlessness."[2]

Lacking a sense of tradition and community, we float in a sea of uncertainty masquerading as the "virtue" of choice. How could we not become anxious and fearful when we lack connection both to our past and to our present? To put it another way, the absence of community—both the community of the dead that we call "tradition" and the community of the living—adds to our fear because it becomes less clear what it looks like to live well, and apart from some such definition, we remain anxious about our choices. The absence of community also leaves us with a sense that our resources are scarce, since we cannot necessarily count on the support of others in difficult times. Indeed, in post-9/11 America we have all the more reason to be disconnected from others, precisely because we have learned to view the stranger as a potential source of terror.

All of this means that we tend to lack courage just to the extent that we lack community. As a community we can often bear risks together that we might be reticent to face alone. So if we are to recover courageous living, we need to recover the kind of community capable of supporting it. A community of religious brothers in Taizé, France, has recently provided a remarkable witness to just such communal courage in a fearful world.

Taizé: A Parable of Courage in Community

On Tuesday, August 16, 2005, Brother Roger, the founder and prior of a religious community in Taizé, France, was stabbed to death during a prayer service. As the worshipers sang and the brothers kneeled, a mentally unstable Romanian woman, Luminita Solcan, emerged from the congregation and murdered the ninety-year-old Brother Roger in his wheelchair. The community was shocked and saddened, as were all those who had become friends of Taizé over the years.

The Taizé community was founded in 1940, when Brother Roger sought to create a sanctuary in southern France to assist refugees, Jews and non-Jews, during World War II. Over the years Taizé has grown into an ecumenical monastic community of over a hundred brothers, both Catholic and Protestant. No one who visits Taizé can fail to be moved by the bonds of community that are created, not only among the brothers but also among the thousands of people each year who make pilgrimage to this small French town.

I remember my first visit to Taizé in the summer of 1990. I took a youth group from my church, and we spent a week in prayer, song, reflection, and fellowship. One of the most remarkable aspects of our visit was the opportunity to meet and converse with other young pilgrims from all over the world. We knew almost immediately that our faith linked us to these fellow Christians in a way that broke down boundaries of race, tribe, and nation. A large group from Poland had arrived just before we did, so during that week the community often sang in Polish—a difficult language for English speakers to read. We quickly gave up trying to decipher the words and began to learn the songs by ear, letting ourselves settle into the repetitive rhythms. Soon we were singing along, not always sure what we were saying, but knowing that we were united with our brothers and sisters through Christ in a kind of Pentecost moment—breaking barriers of language, setting Babel at bay.

Being a community of reconciliation, where moments such as these happen day after day, week after week, constitutes the central mission of the brothers. When a new brother makes a lifelong commitment to the community, the service includes the words, "The Lord Christ . . . has chosen you to be in the Church a sign of brotherly love. It is his will that with your brothers you live the parable of community."[3] This metaphor, "parable of community," has become one of the most prominent self-descriptions of Taizé. They seek to enact God's peace and reconciliation on earth as a parabolic witness to the world.

Alongside "parable of community," one often hears Taizé described as a "pilgrimage of trust on earth," a phrase coined by Brother Roger. This has become the theme of yearly gatherings, which over the last twenty-eight years have brought together over 50,000 people, mostly young adults, from all over the world to pray, contemplate, converse, and embrace Brother Roger's vision of trust. Community and trust, two things that are often missing in today's world, define for this community the core of its mission. We learn to trust as we learn to embrace community; that is, the support of the larger body helps us become people who can risk enough to trust.

So, how did the murder of Brother Roger affect the life and mission of Taizé? How could the community sustain its mission when the trust they preach had been broken in the most violent way imaginable? Otto Selles, a professor in the French department at Calvin College, tells of his experience with the brothers a few months after the attack on Brother Roger. Selles had planned to bring nineteen students from Calvin to Taizé during the fall term following the attack. Upon hearing the news of Brother Roger's murder, he became concerned that this event might change the character of Taizé, creating an atmosphere of fear and suspicion.

> Would the community's spirit be broken? And practically, would Taizé restrict access to the Brothers? "Nothing at Taizé has changed. There is no security," said Brother Jean-Marie, when my group finally arrived in lower Burgundy for a very chilly November weekend retreat at Taizé. . . . And while the community continues to grieve Brother Roger's death, he stressed that "the community is very, very united." . . . After the visit, I realized why the Brothers would probably never put metal detectors in the Church of Reconciliation—their sense of spiritual security and calm goes miles deeper than most of us would like to admit. At the funeral service for Brother Roger, Brother Aloïs didn't shy from mentioning Luminita Solcan's name and committing her to God's forgiveness. . . . Set on such a path of both reconciliation and truth, Taizé continues to offer a "parable of community" to France and the rest of the world.[4]

In the midst of these anxious times, we need all the more to attend to that parable of community. Like the parables of Jesus, this band of brothers functions to subvert our easy expectations about how the world works.

Just as the surprising grace of the father stuns us in the parable of the prodigal son, just as the imprudent generosity of the employer shocks us in the parable of the workers in the vineyard, so the simple resumption of a life of community and trust surprises us in the lived parable of Taizé. "There is no security," says Brother Jean-Marie. No security? The founder of the community has just been stabbed to death during worship by a woman who carried in a knife for this very purpose. Surely some metal detectors would be in order? Surely some process of screening the visitors would be sensible? But parables do not exist to reinforce our assumptions about caution and common sense. They put us face to face with God's profound grace and urge us to take the profound risk of loving the other as God does.

The parable of community in Taizé reveals another path to walk for the rest of us, who, whether from real danger or manipulated fear, also feel violated and vulnerable. Like any good parable, the life of the brothers stretches our imaginations, and by simply returning to their open, hospitable life of trust, they make possible a response to evil that many of us would have thought impossible. I imagine part of what makes such courage possible is that fear is borne collectively by the community. Thus, their courage is expressed as a communal virtue. The apostle Paul tells us to "bear one another's burdens" (Gal. 6:2). In a fearful world, one of the most profound ways we can do this for each other is to create a community where our fears, our risks, and our resources can be shared in common.

The remainder of this chapter focuses on the connection between community and courage, but first, we would do well to answer some basic questions—what is courage and how do we distinguish courage from recklessness?

What Is Courage?

Courage is the capacity to do what is right and good in the face of fear. We become courageous when we learn to live for something that is more important than our own safety. The Taizé community, for instance, exists not for self-preservation (individually or corporately) but to give the world a taste of God's kingdom. Hence, for them, courage takes the form of living their life of hospitality and reconciliation even when they feel threatened. Jesus showed courage when "he set his face to go to Jerusalem" (Luke 9:51), knowing that he was walking into a religious and political powder keg. Yet he knew that his mission was more important than his safety.

Of course, we might want to ask how we know that the actions of the Taizé community or the boldness of Jesus are "courageous" and not just reckless. If you know that you are a marked man, do you walk straight into a crowded public place and announce yourself by raising a ruckus in the temple? Or if you have once fallen prey to an attack, do you continue with business as usual? Or if you leave your house unlocked and it gets robbed, do you leave it unlocked again? How do we discern the difference between courage and foolishness?

First of all, as discussed in chapter 4, having courage does not mean that you lack fear or that you ignore your fear. As the ancient philosopher Aristotle rightly notes, a person would have to be "a sort of madman or insensible person if he feared nothing" (remember that in the Brothers Grimm story, the boy who was without fear acted like a mad, insensible person). Aristotle goes on, "The man who exceeds in confidence about what really is terrible is rash. The rash man, however, is also thought to be boastful and only a pretender to courage."[5] Feeling no fear at all would make one a "madman," while being excessively confident in the face of fear makes one rash. Neither of these is to be confused with courage. The courageous person feels fear but is not overcome by it. The courageous person recognizes danger but refuses to let fear get in the way of doing what is right, good, and necessary. The courageous person also shows prudence in the face of danger, since prudence (or "practical wisdom") is an important companion virtue to courage. Prudence rightly tells us that there is no virtue in taking the wrong kind of risks. Prudence helps us discern the difference between being rash and having courage.

For instance, is it courageous for a single woman, living alone, to let a homeless man stay overnight in her house? We might say that this borders on being reckless rather than courageous, though such a woman might act out of the best Christian motives. To give another example, I feel no compulsion to pick up a hitchhiker when my young boys are in the car with me. While someone might say this is a failure of courage, letting fear keep me from offering hospitality, prudence tells me that this would be a rash act. Not all risky behavior is courageous, even when it is intended for the good of another. There are some risks that we need not take, since our own lives (and those we love) are gifts from God, and faithfulness calls us to value those gifts. One of the things a Christian community can do for us is provide a place to weigh judgments together about courageous action. The community ought to be a place of discernment, so that we do not need to rely on individual judgments alone.

Community and Courage

The virtue of courage requires that our fears be rightly formed. That is, courage requires feeling the right amount of fear—not so little that we become reckless about our lives, but not so much that we are paralyzed or become viciously defensive. How is it that we "form" our fear? How do we learn to control our fear so that it does not control us? How do we learn to be courageous?

We learn courage pretty much the way we learn everything else—by watching other people. Theologian Paul Wadell has said, "Friendship is the crucible of the moral life,"[6] by which he means that the virtues we need to live well are shaped by sharing a life together with friends who help us become good. Virtues are learned by being with others who embody the virtues. A virtue is different from a rule or a principle, for as with a musical score, you cannot really know what a virtue is like on paper—it has to be performed. We learn to be virtuous by seeing virtuous people act in virtuous ways. Lacking a community in which the virtues are being sought and lived, one would be hard pressed to develop any of the virtues, including courage.

Anglican theologian John Milbank argues that "virtue cannot properly operate except when collectively possessed."[7] This is never truer than when talking about courage. Courage requires community, both for the learning of courage and the living of it. And this community is not just of the present, but of all those who have gone before us. In the reading of scripture and the remembrance of the saints, we recall all those who have embodied courage in the past. We remember them and pray for the strength to imitate them.

Here, the martyrs become especially important, since they embodied the most powerful witness to courage we can imagine. They recognized that discipleship would require risk, but they did not step back from it. They lived for something bigger than self-preservation, so the threat of death could not scare them into unfaithfulness. They were sustained by communities that not only taught them courage, but promised to tell their stories to future generations, assuring them that their sacrifice would not be forgotten. The courage of the martyr relies upon the courage of a community that dares to keep the martyr's story alive. Today more than ever, our churches need to be telling and celebrating these stories. In the case of the Taizé community, Brother Roger's murder makes him a martyr (that is, a "witness") insofar as the brothers tell his story of faithfulness in such a way that it sustains their own courage in the face of similar danger.

Of course, it is possible that a Christian community's life will not support and sustain courage but rather work against it. Over time a church can settle into patterns of institutional life that turn the focus inward and tempt a people to become content with self-preservation. Some have called such communities "maintenance churches."[8] I have been involved with more than one church over the years that seemed to have little sense of mission beyond keeping the doors open. There was no courageous reaching out, there was no bold risking of time or resources. Rather, there was careful consideration of how to preserve the good thing we had going. Such churches, while they may offer a great deal to those who attend, could hardly be considered courageous and would be unlikely places for individuals to develop the virtue of courage, since the temptation to self-preservation so quickly shuts down courageous action.

Giving Words to Fear

Developing the virtue of courage requires not only a community that embodies and remembers courage, but a community in which our fears can be given voice. Too often even church (maybe especially church) can be a place where we feel the need to hide our fears, to "dress up" so that we become presentable to God and others. This usually requires hiding the dark stuff underneath a smile and a handshake. We are not often good at making vulnerable confessions, and church can, unfortunately, be a place where vulnerability is met with either judgment or platitudes. And yet, fear grows all the more powerful when we cannot speak it. To give words to our fear, to name our fear, is to begin to dispel its power.

This truth is pointed out wonderfully in the novel *Life of Pi,* by Yan Martel. The main character, Piscine Patel, known as Pi, lives in Pondicherry, India, with a literary mother and a rationalist father. To the chagrin of both his parents, Pi seems to be inescapably religious (he practices Christianity, Islam, and Hinduism all at the same time). Pi's father runs the zoo in Pondicherry, until the money dries up and he decides to move. The family and some of the remaining zoo animals board a Japanese ship headed to Canada, but on the way the ship sinks. The only survivors are Pi and a 450-pound Bengal tiger named Richard Parker. They share a twenty-six-foot lifeboat and for 227 days drift through a series of adventures, real and imagined, hoping for shore or rescue. While on the boat Pi begins to reflect on his fears (alternately the fear of dying at sea and the fear of being eaten by Richard Parker). His analysis of how fear works is worth quoting at length.

> I must say a word about fear. It is life's only true opponent. Only fear can defeat life. It is a clever, treacherous adversary, how well I know. It has no decency, respects no law or convention, shows no mercy. It goes for your weakest spot, which it finds with unerring ease. It begins in your mind, always. One moment you are feeling calm, self-possessed, happy. Then fear, disguised in the garb of mild-mannered doubt, slips into your mind like a spy. Doubt meets disbelief and disbelief tries to push it out. But disbelief is a poorly armed foot soldier. Doubt does away with it with little trouble. You become anxious. Reason comes to do battle for you. You are reas-

sured. Reason is fully equipped with the latest weapons technology. But, to your amazement, despite superior tactics and a number of undeniable victories, reason is laid low. You feel yourself weakening, wavering. Your anxiety becomes dread. Quickly you make rash decisions. You dismiss your last allies: hope and trust. There, you've defeated yourself. Fear, which is but an impression, has triumphed over you.

Neither disbelief nor reason, two skills Pi's parents have tried to teach him, can win a battle with fear. Fear, being an emotion, is not amenable to rational argument, nor can it be forced out by mere negation. His judgment that fear is "but an impression" echoes Aquinas's description of fear as an act of the imagination. Yet locating fear in the imagination does not make it any less real. It only highlights its specterlike quality, its ability to evade the grasp that would subdue it. Once disbelief and reason fail to fend off fear, one makes the rash decision to dismiss hope and trust. These are, according to Pi, one's "last allies." But how can one avoid that rash decision, that pit-of-the-stomach sense of inevitability that causes a person to throw in the towel, to lose hope and give up trust? Pi concludes with this bit of wisdom:

> The matter is difficult to put into words. For fear, real fear, such as shakes you to your foundation, such as you feel when you are brought face to face with your mortal end, nestles in your memory like a gangrene; it seeks to rot everything, even the words with which to speak of it. So you must fight hard to express it. You must fight hard to shine the light of words upon it. Because if you don't, if your fear becomes a wordless darkness that you avoid, perhaps even manage to forget, you open yourself to further attacks of fear because you never truly fought the opponent who defeated you.[9]

Words remain Pi's only tool to ward off fear. Fear grows strongest when we allow it to fester as a "wordless darkness." Words not only help us understand our fear but, more importantly, make it possible to share fear. To speak our fear to another is to begin to loosen the grip that fear has on us. To make fear take form in speech is to name it as something that can be confronted, not confronted alone but in the community of those willing to speak their fears aloud and thus begin to subdue them.

This, of course, leads us back to the importance of community, specifically the church. The church, the body of Christ, is that place where, through baptism, we have already faced death, our greatest fear, and seen it overcome. And so we ought to exist as a gathering in which fears can be expressed honestly, since we no longer believe they can control us. If giving voice to fear is one way of keeping fear from controlling us, then the church needs to become a place where we are not embarrassed to hear the fears of others or to share our own. Indeed, it needs to become a place that helps us find the words to bring fear out of the "wordless darkness." This may happen through small groups and support groups where we come to know and trust one another well enough to share our fears. It may happen through the liturgy, especially the psalms of lament, which allow us to give voice together to our fears and anxieties. It may happen in the proclamation, as preachers name from the pulpit the fears that grip us. And when it does happen, we will begin to become communities of courage precisely because we have found ways to name, and thus confront, the fears that keep us from living fully and joyfully.

Sharing Risks and Resources

Someone might respond to this last section by saying it's all fine and good to talk about fear, but if we have no resources to defend against it, our words will be empty. And there is some truth to this. Having courage requires not just a community where fear can be spoken, but a community in which our risks and our resources can be shared in common. As we noted in the last chapter, we tend to fear more when we have less. This becomes an even more pressing issue in the context of Christian discipleship, for Jesus models a life in which certain resources are relinquished. For instance, Jesus challenges our attempts to find security in wealth or power. He deflates the ambitions of those disciples who, after the Last Supper, argue over who will hold the highest position in Jesus's administration. He says to them, "The kings of the Gentiles lord it over them; and those in authority over them are called benefactors. But not so with you; rather the greatest among you must become like the youngest, and the leader like one who serves" (Luke 22:25–26). Jesus redefines power and relativizes riches. In so doing, he asks his followers to relinquish certain kinds of resources that could be used to ward off threats and dangers. In other words, he makes our lives potentially more dangerous and thus more fearful. Yet he also calls his community of followers into a shared life in which no one has to have all the resources to meet threats and dangers, since the resources of the whole community are at the disposal of anyone in need. What is lost in terms of goods accumulated for one's own security is gained back in terms of a communal network of shared risk and resource.

This strikes me as the real point of the communal sharing that happened in the Book of Acts. Early Christians interpreted Jesus's call to relinquish wealth not as a demand for absolute poverty, but as a decision to open all of their resources to the needs of others in the community. So, rather than becoming poorer, everyone became richer. Luke, the writer of Acts, describes the community this way: "All who believed were together and had all things in common; they would sell their possessions and goods and distribute the proceeds to all, as any had need" (Acts 2:44–45). Thus, "there was not a needy person among them" (Acts 4:34). Though the book of Acts may at times idealize the early church, it gives us a vision of shared risk and resources that could be very helpful for overcoming fear. If I really believed that if I lost my job or my child got sick, I would not have to respond on my own, then I might fear the future less. If I really believed that the resources of my community were open to me in case of an emergency, then I might fear the emergency less. If I really believed that my community would support my family if I got arrested protesting for peace, then I might be more likely to summon the courage and take a stand.

In his reflections on friendship and risk, Paul Wadell makes the observation that "it is much easier to take the risk of loving someone when we know we are loved and cherished by another."[10] In other words, the presence of a loving community makes it easier to take the risk of extending love to someone outside the community. Here we come back to the connection of hospitality and courage with which we began the chapter. The brothers of Taizé are able to take the risk of loving and welcoming the stranger, even the potentially dangerous stranger, because they share a common life in which their common love supports the extension of that love to others. And though such love can be risky, as Brother Roger's murder powerfully underscored, the risks of such actions are not borne by one individual alone. There can be no solution to the problem of fear without the existence of communities capable of bearing fear together.

Questions for Discussion

1. Imagine yourself as one of the brothers in the Taizé community. After Brother Roger's death, would you find it difficult to return to life as usual without enacting special safeguards and security measures? Do you think you would feel fearful every time you were gathered for worship? What do you think makes it possible for them to live so courageously?
2. Can you think of an example of someone doing something really courageous that impressed you (no, the woman who ate a bowlful of worms on *Fear Factor* doesn't count—I mean something *really* courageous)? What made the act courageous and not just reckless?
3. Do you agree that our competitive and individualistic culture isolates us and thus makes us more afraid? If so, what do you think it will take to restore community? Have you ever experienced a church that really acted like a community of friends?

4. This chapter uses *Life of Pi* to help us think about fear. If you have read the book, can you think of other aspects of the story that speak to fear, faith, and courage? Can you think of other stories, novels, or movies that give insights into fear or courage?

5. Have you ever heard of (or been a part of) a church in which the members actually offered tangible support (goods and money) to one another as needed? Do you think it could happen? What would it take?

6

Narrative and Providence

■ Our communities can press forward in the face of fear not only because we share risks and resources in common, but also because we tell certain stories that give us hope. In Christian communities we tell stories of God's provision—like the time God provided a ram for Abraham to sacrifice instead of Isaac, like the time God provided manna (a breadlike substance) in the desert to sustain the Israelites on their journey, like the time God provided the Holy Spirit to a fearful group of disciples on Pentecost. In theological terms, we call this pattern of divine provision "providence" (which, of course, contains the root word *provide*). Providence is our ongoing affirmation of Abraham's words on Mount Moriah, "the Lord will provide" (Gen. 22:14). But to be honest, many of us today find it more difficult to trust in God's providence than did those who lived in earlier times.

In this chapter I try to understand why this is. I trace some of the changes that have occurred over the last few centuries that have made it more difficult for many of us to believe in divine providence. Our response to these changes, to this "liberal" shift that no longer sees God in the world, need not be a return to premodern thought, to a "conservative" belief that God is everywhere and the cause of all events. Rather, we need to find a third way that gets beyond the liberal/conservative divide. I would suggest we do this by approaching providence through a narrative lens, focusing on the ways the stories of our lives intersect with the stories of scripture. Thus, narration becomes more important than explanation, and purpose becomes more important than causality. In other words, we may come to see providence as a way of narrating our lives in light of God's larger purpose rather than as a way of explaining every event as caused by God. This will help us, first, to avoid the problems that come with attributing evil and suffering to God's will, and, second, to reclaim the importance of providence as a way of story-ing the world that gives us hope and courage in fearful times.

Premodern Providence

From the ancient church through the Reformation, Christians encountering danger or threat would have drawn strength from the belief that no matter what happened, God was still the Lord of history. God's will could be seen in all that happened, even if seen only darkly. The reformer John Calvin provides a telling example of the premodern view that God controls all events. For Calvin this conviction produced a comfort that came from knowing that everything was in God's hands. Yet Calvin in no way lived in denial of the evils and dangers that surrounded him. Reflecting a keen sense of the dangers of everyday life, he wrote:

> Innumerable are the evils that beset human life: innumerable, too, the deaths that threaten it. We need not go beyond ourselves: since our body is the receptacle of a thousand diseases—in fact holds within itself and fosters the causes of diseases—a man cannot go about unburdened by many forms of his own destruction, and without drawing out a life enveloped, as it were, with death. For what else would you call it, when he neither freezes nor sweats without danger? Now, wherever you turn, all things around you not only are hardly to be trusted but almost openly menace, and seem to threaten immediate death. Embark upon a ship, you are one step away from death. Mount a horse, if one foot slips, your life is imperiled. Go through the city streets, you are subject to as many dangers as there are tiles on the roofs. . . . Amid these tribulations must not man be most miserable, since, but half alive in life, he weakly draws his anxious and languid breath, as if he had a sword perpetually hanging over his neck?[1]

Calvin gives us a vivid glimpse of what a sixteenth-century version of the culture of fear might look like. Yet in the midst of his robust capacity to imagine future evils, Calvin found peace, because he believed that nothing would happen apart from God's will. Thus, he follows the previous litany of dangers with this affirmation: "Yet, when that light of divine providence has once shone upon a godly man, he is then relieved and set free not only from the extreme anxiety and fear that were pressing him before, but from every care."[2] Divine providence was, for Calvin, the affirmation that all things, big and small, flow from the will of God and therefore serve God's good purposes, even if we cannot understand those purposes. The strong affirmation that God acts in the world to sustain, accompany, and guide the creation provided for premodern Christians a foundation for life.

And yet, such a conviction as Calvin's brought with it a host of theological difficulties. Note that for Calvin we are set free from anxiety and fear not because we believe God will protect us from all danger, but because we know that all that happens reflects God's will and serves God's plan. The sufferings and horrors of the modern era, however, including the Holocaust, the World Wars, and the atomic bomb, have made such a conviction untenable for many Christians. How can we say that such evils are God's will? Why would God plan a world that included the mass murder of his chosen people? How could we possibly worship a God who wills the torture of children? While Calvin managed to draw comfort from his belief in a comprehensive divine plan, few of us today find such a belief comforting. We are more likely to be repulsed by it. How did things change?

The Loss of Providence

The demise of the doctrine of providence followed in many ways the loss of story in the modern world (for more on this, see the appendix). During the seventeenth and eighteenth centuries, modern science and historical studies gave us purely natural explanations of world events, making it no longer necessary to appeal to God to make sense of the world. At the same time, traditional religious authorities, such as the Bible and the church's traditions, were being called into question. Interestingly, belief in providence did not immediately disappear; instead, for a time, it became even more important. Christians needed a way to make belief in God reasonable in an age of rationality, and by pointing to the ordering of nature and human progress, they believed they could prove the existence of an all-powerful designer of the plan. Providence was thus reduced to a conviction that could be read off of nature itself and did not require engagement with the biblical stories. This turn away from scripture and tradition to "natural theology" proved to be a fateful and ultimately flawed theological decision.

For many in Europe the conviction that nature and history showed God's hand at work was profoundly challenged by the Lisbon earthquake (and the ensuing tsunami and fires) of 1755, which killed between 60,000 and 100,000 people along the coast of Portugal and provoked an outcry of theological questions. Where was God? How could God let this happen? How could this be God's will? The fact that the earthquake occurred on All Saints Day as Christians throughout Lisbon were gathering for worship provided a perverse theological postscript to the disaster.

This marked an erosion of belief in providence that continued into the nineteenth century. In 1859 Charles Darwin published *Origin of the Species*.[3] His hypothesis that all living creatures evolved from less complex to more complex beings devastated the proponents of natural theology, because they had assumed that divine planning was the only way to account for the order found in nature (this was the precursor to the contemporary argument about "intelligent design"). If a certain animal were perfectly adapted to live and thrive in a certain environment, this was seen by the natural theologians as a sign that God had perfectly planned the elements of creation to fit together. Suddenly, with Darwin, another explanation emerged. The mutually beneficial ecosystems in which animals and plants sustain each other, while appearing on the surface to require an intelligent designer, could actually be explained by adaptation and natural selection. Those living creatures that survived over the long haul did so by adapting to their environment. Positive adaptations increased the chance of survival, while less beneficial mutations made it less likely for a creature to survive. Thus, the survivors were necessarily adapted to their environment in a way that presented a sense of order and pattern but which did not necessarily imply a Creator.

By providing an alternative account of the order of things, Darwin exploited the weak foundation on which the natural theologians had built their house. Indeed, their house of faith turned out to be a house of cards. One need not make Darwin an enemy, for the natural theologians had already sealed their fate when they opted for *apologetics,* the attempt to prove Christianity to modern skeptics, over *witness,* the attempt to live in such a way that God's true story becomes visible and attractive to the world. Seeking to make belief in God universally acceptable, indeed universally unassailable, the natural theologians overstepped their bounds, and, like Icarus, with his wings of wax, eventually came crashing to the ground. This, however, did not mean the end of providence.

The doctrine made a comeback in the period after Darwin, not as a rival theory to evolution but as an explanation of evolution itself. God was invoked as the "God of the gaps," the cosmic director of the evolutionary process, whose intervention was invoked to explain ruptures in the chain of evolution. But as with the natural theology of the seventeenth and eighteenth centuries, this attempt to make God necessary according to science would last only as long as there were evolutionary questions that science could not explain. The "God of the gaps" would inevitably be dismissed when the gaps were closed. We should not be surprised that by the middle of the twentieth century, providence was increasingly ignored in theological conversations. Christians found it ever more difficult to describe God's action in the world in a way that could even approximate the certainty of premodern times.

Finding the Story

How, then, might we reformulate our understanding of providence to name our conviction that our futures can be trusted to God's care, even when we cannot believe that God is the direct cause of all that happens? How can providence become a source of strength and courage in a culture of fear? To do this will mean shifting our emphasis from trying to create an explanation of suffering and evil to creating an interpretation of suffering and evil. In other words, we need to shift from a philosophical model in which we try to create the right concepts and propositions to a literary model where we try to get the story right. Providence, at its heart, has to do with the conviction that our lives and our world constitute a coherent story, a drama, in which God and humankind, together, drive the story toward its proper conclusion. Of course, human beings often fail to participate faithfully in the drama. We often act in ways that hinder the progress of the story. We often make such a mess of things that it is no longer clear that there is a story at all; thus, we often experience our lives as randomness and chaos. Providence is the conviction that through it all God's story cannot be lost, and thus God's hopes for the human story cannot be thwarted.

Isak Dinesen, author of *Out of Africa*, once said, "All sorrows can be borne, if you put them into a story."[4] I suspect what she meant by this was that hope and even healing can come from finding form in the midst of chaotic wanderings. Narrative gives form to suffering, which on its own tends toward fragmentation. Of course, we must not be too quick to supplant fragmentation with narrative. In the darkness of suffering, what we need most is not someone trying to make sense of our suffering, but someone willing to recognize that the suffering has broken every structure that once gave order to our lives. Often only in retrospect can we tell the story of our suffering and situate it within a bigger story that makes our suffering something more than hopeless, something more than tragic.

Providence names the belief that ultimately we live in a story in which suffering, and even death, cannot be the last word. Barbara Brown Taylor unpacks Dinesen's words this way: "There is a strange kind of comfort in a story that tells the truth about how bad things can get. . . . Plus, the very fact that someone is telling it means that you are not alone.

Someone else has been there. Someone else knows what it is like, and that company—that communion—can make all the difference."[5] Stories create redemptive order in chaos by drawing us into a community of shared story where we know that our chaos is bounded by the lives of those who surround us.

Reclaiming providence as a way of telling our stories helps us address one of the dominant, though perhaps more subtle, fears of modern and postmodern people—the fear that our lives have no purpose, which is, I think, to say that our lives have no story. Quite apart from the disorientation that comes from suffering, our ordinary lives often seem to lack direction or meaning. We fall into a malaise that can be as destructive as affliction (sometimes more so). We dread the possibility that we have no beginning, middle, or end, no introduction and no conclusion, no unity that would allow us to make our "life story" make sense. We worry that in the end our lives will seem to us and to others but a random assortment of moments, decisions, events, and sufferings.

To borrow a cliché from Forrest Gump, we worry that "life is like a box of chocolates"—not because "you never know what you'll get," but because a box of chocolates is simply consumed piece by random piece until nothing is left. Our lives, we fear, reflect not the unfolding of a story, but the mere consuming of time, so that when we are gone we find the box has not been filled by our living but has been emptied by it.

Figuring Out Providence

To think of providence in terms of narration rather than propositions means that we give up trying to explain exactly *how* God is present in any given event of our lives and histories. Instead, we learn to read our stories and the world's history in a figurative way that finds patterns of divine activity within the seeming chaos of the cosmos. By "figurative," I mean reading one thing in light of another, so that each gains new meaning by being brought together. For instance, Christians have often read certain passages from the Old Testament figuratively. The story of Abraham's near sacrifice of Isaac has long been interpreted as a foreshadowing of Christ's sacrifice on the cross. Each story tells of a father handing over a son for sacrifice, and just as Isaac carried on his back the wood for the burnt offering, so Jesus carried the cross for his execution. Though Abraham did not have to sacrifice his son, God the Father in the Gospels does, in fact, give his Son to be sacrificed. This is one "figurative" way of reading the two stories in light of each other. Another way to "figure" the stories is to see Jesus not as Isaac but as the ram that takes Isaac's place. Here we see Jesus as the one who is sacrificed in the place of all the Isaacs, the one whose death puts an end to sacrifice. Each of these interpretations is figurative, reading one story in light of another.

The fact that we might figure the relationship between these two stories in more than one way alerts us to the fact that figuration is not a science but an art. Figurations of both text and history are neither hard-and-fast nor exclusive, but rather are patient of refiguring and even multiple simultaneous interpretations. The process of interpreting God's activity is never finished. It is ongoing and often requires reinterpretation as new events unfold. Thus, we preserve the mystery of divine providence while remaining confident that God will bring human history (and the whole cosmos) to its good and proper end.

The practice of reading world history in light of the stories of the Bible relies on Christians developing the skill to see the world through the lens of scripture, connecting events in the present to patterns of divine activity in the Bible. For example, in the fourth century the Christian historian Eusebius figuratively interpreted the first Christian emperor of Rome, Constantine, as a new Moses, imagining that he was going to lead God's people to a new promised land. But by the next century, Augustine, a bishop and theologian, painted a very different picture of the Roman Empire, even in its Christian form. He interpreted its history as the unfolding violent repetition of its founding story of fratricide. As the myth goes, Romulus and Remus were sons of Mars, the god of war, raised by a she-wolf in the wilderness and destined to found Rome. But upon founding the city, Romulus killed Remus, named the city after himself, and became its first ruler. Augustine interpreted this story in a figurative relation to the biblical narrative of Cain and Abel, thus connecting the founding of Rome to the Christian story of sin, murder, and betrayal. Just as Cain killed Abel and ushered in a reign of violence, so Romulus's murder of Remus placed the Roman Empire on the side of sinful, murderous power rather than on the side of God. Thus, the fall of the Roman Empire could be understood by Augustine as God's proper judgment on a people who, from the start, stood for violence rather than peace.

Literary critic Erich Auerbach makes the case that this biblical and early church pattern of reading history figuratively introduced something radically new to the way history had been interpreted before.[6]

> For example, if an occurrence like the sacrifice of Isaac is interpreted as prefiguring the sacrifice of Christ, so that in the former the latter is as it were announced and promised, and the latter "fulfills" . . . the former, then a connection is established between two events which are linked neither temporally nor causally—a connection which it is impossible to establish by reason in the horizontal dimension (if I may be permitted to use this term for a temporal extension). It can be established only if both occurrences are

81

vertically linked to Divine Providence, which alone is able to devise such a plan of history and supply the key to its understanding.[7]

So, the connection between two events, in this case two events within the Bible, lies not in a temporal connection (they did not happen at or near the same time, nor in a causal chain): the binding of Isaac was not a contributing "cause" to the death of Jesus centuries later. Rather, the connection is that both stories point us to some "vertical" connection, a pattern of how God works in history.

This becomes a way of reading not just stories but current events. Auerbach goes on to spell out these consequences: "The here and now is no longer a mere link in an earthly chain of events, it is simultaneously something which has always been, and which will be fulfilled in the future; and strictly, in the eyes of God, it is something eternal, something omni-temporal, something already consummated in the realm of fragmentary earthly event."[8] The capacity of figurative interpretation to reveal truth about God and the world rests in the belief that God is, in fact, guiding human history, and therefore the figurative connections are not arbitrary but are evidence of a divine pattern of activity.

Auerbach adds that such figuration "by no means signifies a devaluation of life on earth or of human individuality; but it did bring with it a blunting of tragic climaxes here on earth."[9] Each event, each person's story remains important, but its importance is enhanced when it becomes a sign of God's story that stretches from creation to consummation. And in God's story, the final word is life. For Jews the primary story that bears witness to this truth is the Exodus.[10] For Christians that pivotal story is Jesus's death and resurrection. The stories are "paradigms" in the sense that we say of them, "here's a story that shows how God works"—not just how God *worked* in the past, but how God *works* in the present. God does not leave Israel enslaved, God does not leave Jesus in the grave, God does not leave us in our suffering and sorrow. And so, if these stories reflect God's determination not to let death win, then, as Auerbach said, there is a "blunting of tragic climaxes here on earth." In God's story, no earthly event can be finally and utterly tragic. This is the deep truth of the Christian belief in providence.

Pattern Recognition

We might say that figurative reading, and thus the capacity to see and affirm divine providence in history, requires learning the art of "pattern recognition." In a recent novel by that name, William Gibson, the science-fiction author who coined the term *cyberspace,* explores the ways our fragmented postmodern culture cries out for those who are able to find pattern in the pieces. The main character of the novel, Cayce Pollard, exhibits a talent for "cool hunting," an ability to recognize repeatable patterns of "cool" as they arise within youth subcultures. She works as a market researcher helping corporations discover, brand, and cash in on this embryonic coolness. Her ability to perceive the patterns of emerging trends makes her the right person to tackle the mystery of 135 film clips that have been anonymously posted on the Internet. The release of these clips, one by one, has over time created a cult following linked by a message board, "Fetish: Footage: Forum," on which enthusiasts from around the world try to decipher the seemingly random scenes.

Pattern Recognition suggests there is more than one way to make something of the disconnected pieces of culture. On the one hand, we might ferret through the fragments (cool hunting) in order to profit from emerging trends (pattern recognition as a money-making enterprise). On the other hand, we might explore the apparently random pieces of life and culture (the film clips) in order to gain greater understanding of how things just might hold together (pattern recognition as an identity-making enterprise). In this story Pollard stands at the center of both endeavors. She makes use of her uncanny intuitions about branding in order to make big bucks from (and for) the multinationals, all the while spending her real energy trying to unravel the connection between the film clips and her father's mysterious disappearance.

As I read this novel I could not help but think that its investigation of "pattern recognition" provided a fruitful metaphor for figurative interpretation and divine providence. Like Cayce Pollard seeking a narrative structure in the 135 film clips, Christians look for a unified plotline that holds together the seemingly fragmented events of our lives and our world. To speak of divine providence as pattern recognition does not mean that we reduce all the loose ends of historical reality to a finely packaged formula (the kind of tidy ending that Gibson's book itself refuses to give). From our place within the story, we cannot give an account of everything; thus, certain things will always remain outside the story we are able to tell. To seek totality in our storytelling would be to assume that we could get a "God's eye view" on things, when in fact our views are always limited and partial. Any attempt to suggest that we have put all the pieces together would force us to distort or exclude the pieces that do not seem to fit, pieces that might, themselves, be hints that we need to figure the pattern differently, perhaps more truthfully.

All we can hope for is a place to stand and a way to move forward in the midst of ongoing negotiations about how to interpret the pattern rightly. Only in God's time will we see how it all holds together (or perhaps we will see that "holding together" is the wrong metaphor). Yale theologian Hans Frei has put the matter well:

> In this respect, as in so many others, we see in a glass darkly. But seeing darkly is not the same as discerning nothing at all. Abiding mystery is not identical with absolute unintelligibility. In our endeavor to narrate the as-yet-unfinished pattern of history, we reach for parables that might serve to set forth a kind of pattern, though not to confine history and the mysterious providence of God to these symbolic meanings. Sequences of events differ from each other sufficiently widely and always take place in a sufficiently unexpected manner so that we cannot claim that any set of images or parables can give us *the* clue to the pattern of history.[11]

We tie up what we can while acknowledging loose ends; we discern something of the pattern while recognizing that the pattern as a whole may be deeper and more complex than we ever imagined.

Suffering, Pattern, and Providence

So, how might "providence as pattern recognition" work in practice? In a particularly powerful passage of his book *Night,* Elie Wiesel tells of the attempts made by several Jews in Auschwitz to make sense of their suffering in relation to their faith.[12] He notes that some of his fellow inmates interpreted their suffering in terms of the biblical pattern of exile. That is, just as the Jews were punished by God with exile in the sixth century BCE, so God was punishing the Jews of Germany for their failure to follow Torah. Others rejected the idea that the Nazi horror could be God's punishment, turning instead to other biblical patterns of divine action. Akiba Drumer suggested that God was testing the Jews to discover the strength and purity of their faith, just as God tested Abraham. A third prisoner, Hersch Genud, suggested that the only way to understand what was happening was to see it as the end of the world, drawing on the biblical imagery of apocalypse. Wiesel interpreted his suffering through the lens of Job. He cried out to God, lamented, and raged, just as Job did. He decried the suffering of the innocents just as Job did. He did not doubt God's existence, but he came to doubt God's justice. Yet even as Wiesel voiced his complaint, he placed himself not outside Judaism but within the Jewish biblical pattern of lament.

Each of these men struggled to see the horrific sufferings of the Holocaust in a figurative relationship to some biblical story, some pattern of divine activity that, though it would not *explain* the suffering, would place the suffering in a *narrative* that would not render it hopeless. Each of these paradigmatic narratives gave the men hope that for them the story was not over. Each of these biblical stories ended not with a final destruction but with deliverance and redemption—God leads the Jews back from exile to rebuild the temple, God stays Abraham's hand to preserve Isaac's life, God redeems the apocalyptic end by the coming of the Messiah, and God appears to Job to restore his fortunes. The ability to narrate one's story in relation to a biblical story can provide hope that even suffering, even death, will not be the last word for God's people.

About ten years ago some good friends of mine were expecting their second child. We all looked forward to welcoming this new life and celebrating together. But when the baby girl, Lucy, was born, physicians discovered she had a birth defect called osteogenesis imperfecta, type II. This defect, the parents were told, was "not compatible with life." Lucy lived only a few hours. The hopes and dreams that the parents held for this child were crushed, and we all shared in their sadness. A few weeks later we received a birth/death announcement. The small card bore the imprint of Lucy's foot. It noted her time of birth and time of death. Inside were the words, "The Lord gave, and the Lord has taken away; blessed be the name of the Lord" (Job 1:21). The words were hard to read, not just because of my tears, but because I found it hard to believe that Lucy had been "taken away" by the Lord. Why would God have knit together this new life only to end it so abruptly? But I quickly realized that this was not the right question to be asking. These faithful parents were not so much making a theological claim about how God took their child. Rather they were narrating their loss in terms of the biblical story of Job, an innocent man who suffered and demanded from God an explanation. They were figuratively placing themselves in the shoes of Job, crying out in pain, yet holding fast to their faith and commending their daughter to God's hands. They saw in their own lives a pattern of loss and lament that had been repeated by faithful people time after time going back to Jesus on the cross, David in the Psalms, and Job in his lament for lost children.

Such figurative narration helps us to go on. It gives us words when we have no words. It reminds us that we are not alone. It places our pain in a community of pain. It gives us hope to affirm that this pain is not the last word. Just as Job saw God and was restored, so all of us prayed that Lucy and her parents would experience the same. Figurative interpretation of providence is nothing abstract or fancy—just the willingness to find our story in God's story and in so doing to have hope that tragedy is not the end.

Living the Drama

Sam Wells, dean of Duke Chapel, has suggested a particular kind of figurative reading of the Christian story, a certain way of incorporating

85

the present into the pattern of the biblical world.[13] Using the analogy of a five-act play, Wells interprets the present day as the fourth act in God's drama. The first is God's creation of the world. The second is God's calling of Israel. The third is God's incarnation in Jesus Christ. The fourth is the calling and sending of the church. The fifth is God's culmination of the story in the reign of God.

We live in act four. We live in a time in which church and Israel seek to follow God's calling in anticipation of the coming end (the fifth act)—the fulfillment of time and history in a new heaven and a new earth. Wells suggests that for us to continue the drama we have to know well enough what has happened in the story up until now (scripture and tradition) that we can embody the normative patterns of the biblical stories (such as Exodus and Sinai or cross and resurrection) as we move ahead. Yet we do not have the burden placed on us to make the drama turn out right. Act five lies in God's hands, not ours.

So, how does this relate to providence and fear? As I noted earlier, many people today fear that their lives have no purpose and no goal beyond whatever they may choose to seek in the moment. We fear that all of these individual choices may not add up to much when all is said and done. We sense the burden of giving our lives meaning but fear that all we really have is a series of disconnected choices. But if providence is a way of naming the fact that God has given the world a story and has called each of us to participate in that story, then we are freed from the burden of giving our lives meaning and purpose. Rather we are invited to participate in a meaning that we did not create but which, in fact, created us. In this way we are freed from the fear that comes from having to write our own story, and we are invited to continue the story, to enact the drama, of God's providence.

As Wells puts it, in baptism Christians "move from trying to realize all meaning in their own lives to receiving the heritage of faith and the hope of glory. They move from fearing their fate to singing of their destiny. For this is the effect of God's story: it transforms fate into destiny."[14] Once we begin to see our lives this way, we can begin to welcome the surprising and the unexpected without fear, since we know that God can weave even the darkest turns of history into the ultimate unfolding of God's good end. This is not to say that God *causes* these dark turns—God is not the author of evil. It is to say, rather, that even the darkness cannot rob our lives of purpose, since ultimately our purpose is not constructed but received. What we need, then, are communities that can help us receive and interpret these events in such a way that we "transform fate into destiny." We refuse to name contingency as fate, because we believe that in all things God can and does work for good; in all things God invites us to receive the provision we need to go on; in all things God assures us that evil cannot have the final word.

One of my favorite writers, Flannery O'Connor, transformed her fate into destiny as she wrestled with lupus, a debilitating autoimmune disease. She died of the disease at the age of thirty-nine. As a devout Catholic, she once described her struggle this way: "I have a disease called lupus and I take a medicine called ACTH and I manage well enough to live with both. Lupus is one of those things in the rheumatic department; it comes and goes, I venture forth. My father had it some twelve or fifteen years ago, but at the time there was nothing for it but the undertaker; now it can be controlled with the ACTH. I have enough energy to write with and as that is all I have any business doing anyhow, I can with one eye squinted take it all as a blessing. What you measure out, you come to observe closer, or so I tell myself."[15] O'Connor is able to find blessing in her suffering, though only "with one eye squinted." Looked at directly, with eyes wide open, her illness could be construed as nothing but tragic. Yet, as a writer, she recognizes the gift that comes from seeing more closely the life that is being "measured out" by her illness. In some ways our capacity to see the providing and redeeming work of providence requires this ability to look with squinted eye, to see what the world does not see.

Perhaps it is by such seeing that my friend Bob can make the audacious claim that the stroke he suffered at age twenty-six was "the best thing that ever happened to me." The stroke was part of a series of tragedies that began with his grandmother's death, continued with his mother's death from cancer, and culminated, within a year, in the stroke. These sufferings could easily have brought him to a place of hopeless grieving. They could have left him angry, bitter, and blaming God. In fact, I would not be surprised by such a reaction. And so, the first time he told me that "the stroke was the best thing that ever happened to me," I found it hard to believe. How could such an awful, life-altering experience be thought of, even in retrospect, as good? When I asked him this question, he told me that the stroke was a crucial turning point for him, a kind of wake-up call in which he realized he had to begin to take seriously his life, his faith, and his future. The stroke set Bob on a path that he later would realize was for him a path of life, despite the fact that he would always bear in his body the effects of the stroke. In his willingness to receive the stroke as part of his story, yet not lose faith in the future, Bob transformed fate into destiny.

The capacity to find and accept the good that can come even in suffering reflects a kind of interpretation that can be made only by the person going through the struggle. Rarely can someone else suggest such an interpretation without appearing to trivialize the struggle. Platitudes like "It's all for the best" or "God has his reasons" may be offered sincerely, but they fail to wrestle honestly with the rupture that has occurred in the suffering person's life (I'm reminded of the scene from *Life of Brian* when Brian sings "always look on the bright side of life" while being cruci-fied—a perfect satire of shallow optimism). What we can do in the face of tragedy is provide communities capable of sustaining those who suffer and of receiving their grief, so that they can, over time, come to see their stories redeemed in God's story.

Questions for Discussion

1. This chapter begins with some examples of biblical stories of God's provision—the ram provided to Abraham on Mount Moriah, the manna provided to Israel in the desert, and the Holy Spirit provided to the fearful disciples. Can you think of other biblical stories of divine provision?

2. How have you understood in the past what Christians mean by "providence"? Has this belief been important for your own faith? If so, in what ways?

3. Do you find it hard to believe that God causes everything that hap-pens (even evil and suffering), or does Calvin's traditional belief in providence still make sense to you?

4. How can thinking about providence as a story help us get beyond the problem of either attributing evil to God (the classical view) or saying that God is not involved in this world at all (the modern secular view)?

5. What do you make of Isak Dinesen's claim that "All sorrows can be borne, if you put them into a story"? What do you think she means? Do you think she is right?

6. Have you ever gone through a difficult time in your life in which you were able to "turn fate into destiny" (that is, to accept with hope something that on the surface seemed only tragic)? Did it help to think about your own situation in light of a biblical story (like the characters in Wiesel's *Night* or my friends whose child died)?

7

Security and Vulnerability

■ In the previous chapter we discussed the importance of thinking about providence in narrative terms. Rather than trying to explain how God is (or is not) active in every event in history, we seek to narrate history as a story in which its ultimate progress toward God becomes visible. In so doing, we affirm that history is not just a series of disconnected moments and events. We affirm that each of our lives will finally be drawn into God's story so that our place in that story becomes clear—not that it will always be clear in the moment but in retrospect as we see what God makes of us. We affirm that the story is not tragic but comic, not in the *funny* sense but in the sense that all will be well, that the good hopes and intentions of the characters will not be foiled. To affirm God's providence in the face of fear is to believe that our stories, as they participate in God's story, cannot ultimately be derailed by illness or accident, evil or suffering. The fifth act has already been written and in Christ has already been enacted.

What remains to be said is that as we journey toward that good end, God promises to provide and to redeem, that is, to give us what we need to go on and to reclaim all that is lost along the way. This is God's providential work. Providence does not mean that here and now in this vulnerable world, God will protect us from pain, harm, and danger. To think about providence as a guaranteed protection plan is to mistake both the real contingencies of life and the kind of power God chooses to use in guiding the creation to its goal. We would be naïve to think that our faith would keep bad things from happening to us or to those we love.

Getting beyond Faith as an Insurance Policy

There are, of course, passages in scripture that seem to promise God's protection for the good and the faithful.

I lift up my eyes to the hills—from where will my help come? My help comes from the Lord, who made heaven and earth. He will not let your foot be moved; he who keeps you will not slumber. He who keeps Israel will neither slumber nor sleep. The Lord is your keeper; the Lord is your shade at your right hand. The sun shall not strike you by day, nor the moon by night. The Lord will keep you from all evil; he will keep your life. The Lord will keep your going out and your coming in from this time on and forevermore. (Psalm 121:1–8)

This psalm presents a certain viewpoint within the Bible that emphasizes divine protection for God's people. This voice shows up elsewhere, notably throughout Psalms and Proverbs; for instance, "Trust in the Lord, and do good; so you will live in the land, and enjoy security" (Ps. 37:3). Here the psalmist seems to promise a simple trade: if we trust God, God will protect us.

Jesus speaks in similar ways when he tells the woman with the hemorrhage, "Daughter, your faith has made you well; go in peace, and be healed of your disease" (Mark 5:34). Because she has faith she is healed (but does that mean the converse also applies—if we are not healed, it is because we did not have faith?).

If we were to take these passages alone, we might come to believe, almost as a guarantee, that if we trust God, God will protect or heal us from all harm. While there is a strand of thought in the Bible that implies this, it is hardly the dominant strand, and on its own it does not give the whole picture. Indeed, on its own it can have terrible theological consequences.

Think, for instance, of the story of Job. After Job has lost his livestock, his children, and his health, his friends come to give comfort. After seven days of silence they begin to speak, reiterating the common wisdom found in Psalms and Proverbs—that the good will flourish and the evil will suffer. Job, however, has not sinned. Job is innocent, yet he suffers. The friends have no theological categories to make sense of such innocent suffering. At the end of the book, God vindicates Job and tells the friends, "My wrath is kindled against you . . . for you have not spoken of me what is right, as my servant Job has" (Job 42:7). The book of Job complicates the issues of suffering and divine protection. Clearly, God does not always deliver the good from suffering; indeed, sometimes it is our goodness itself that leads us to suffer.

Dave, a friend of mine from graduate school, lost his twin brother, Steve, to cancer. While struggling against the aggressive disease, Steve received a letter from a Christian woman telling him that she knew it was God's will for him to be miraculously healed. All he had to do was believe. Far from providing comfort, the letter struck Steve like a hot iron of judgment. If he were not healed, she implied, it would be his own fault. This woman thought of divine providence in terms of control and protection. Because she assumed that God controlled all events, she had to create a justification for God's apparent inaction in this case. Her attempt to keep God blameless led her to place blame on Steve—God was ready to do the right thing if only Steve had enough faith. Though he had become very weak, Steve wanted to write a letter in response, so Dave penned the words that Steve slowly struggled to express:

> I share your faith in the almighty power of God to heal and sustain us. There may be times, though, when God's greatest miracle is not the miracle of physical healing, but the miracle of giving us strength in the face of suffering. Paul wrote in 2 Corinthians 12 that he prayed God would remove a thorn in the flesh, but God answered simply, "My grace is sufficient for thee: for my strength is made perfect in weakness . . . for when I am weak, then am I strong." Also, Jesus prayed in the garden that he might not suffer, but it was God's will, and he faced that suffering with a perfect faith.
>
> As I read the Bible, God's promise is to remove all our suffering in the next life, though not necessarily in this one. In this world, we will sometimes weep, suffer, and die. But in the New Jerusalem, "God shall wipe away all tears from their eyes; and there shall be no more death, neither sorrow, nor crying, neither shall there be any more pain, for the former things are passed away" (Revelation 2:14).
>
> I sincerely hope that if my cancer continues to grow, no one will see it as a failure of my faith in God, but that perhaps people can see me as faithful even if I die while I am still young. I do not claim to understand God's will, but I do know that I am in God's hands, whether in life or in death.[1]

The woman's letter to Steve was an exercise in bad theology, though it may have been written with the best intentions. She mistook God's promise to provide with a guarantee to protect, and once she had done that, she could only lay the blame for Steve's cancer at his own feet. Once she had ruled out the possibility that the cancer could result from chance or misfortune (and her understanding of providence left no room for contingency), she assumed that someone had to be blamed for the illness. This perverse theological form of adding insult to injury results from misunderstanding the connection between providence and security.

Providence does not guarantee protection; rather, it assures us of God's provision (making a way for us to go on) and redemption (restoring what is lost along the way).

In the Gospels, Jesus weighed in on these issues of suffering, sin, and divine activity. He asked his disciples how they would interpret the suffering caused when Pilate killed a group of Galilean Jews while they were offering sacrifice in the temple. Did this happen, he asked, because they were "worse sinners than all other Galileans" (Luke 13:2)? His answer? "No, I tell you." And when eighteen people were killed in the collapse of the tower of Siloam, Jesus asked, "Do you think they were worse offenders than all the others living in Jerusalem?" His answer, again, "No, I tell you" (Luke 13:4–5). And when his disciples came upon a blind man and asked "Rabbi, who sinned, this man or his parents, that he was born blind?" Jesus answered, "Neither" (John 9:2–3). Jesus makes clear that these sufferings and tragedies did not result from sin or lack of faith. These victims did not deserve their deaths or infirmities any more than anyone else. The simplistic equation of suffering and sin, the simplistic belief that God will protect the faithful, runs aground on the rough shore of contingency and undeserved misfortune, but this does not mean that God has abandoned us (which is to say that kitschy Christians could, without contradiction, place a "Sh-t Happens" bumper sticker right next to their "God Is My Co-Pilot" decal).

Provision, Redemption, and Security

Divine providence does not promise "security" in any conventional sense, though in today's world that is what many of us long for. We want promises that we will be safe, and if God won't give them to us, our politicians will. Five years after 9/11 the issue of "security" still dominates political discussion. Even topics like immigration, a hot political concern today, receive a security spin in the public debate (this, though the issue has far more to do with the economics of hiring workers from Mexico and Central America than allowing in potential terrorists from the Middle East). But security often comes at a price that is too high to pay. Only by becoming invulnerable can we find absolute security, and invulnerability can be had only by fencing ourselves off from all danger or destroying everyone and everything that poses a possible threat to our well-being.

The political search for security today relies on the conventional power that comes from strength and wealth. But if we believe the biblical witness, that kind of strength is no strength at all. Referring to the cross of Christ, the apostle Paul tells the Corinthians that "God chose what is weak in the world to shame the strong" (1 Cor. 1:27). He goes on to apply this to himself: "whenever I am weak, then I am strong" (2 Cor. 12:10). This paradoxical reversal of strength and weakness tells us something of God's desire to work through human vulnerability rather than to overcome it. Augustine connects this theme directly to security: "When you [God] are our strong security, that is strength indeed, but when our security is in ourselves, that is but weakness."[2] The weight of the biblical tradition lies with the view that God works through our weakness and that precisely as we seek to be "strong," that is, to rely on our own strength for security, we become weak. Only as we rely on God's strength in our weakness do we find real strength. The gospel narratives display this truth in the passion of Christ. The cross reveals his power, which is the power of vulnerable love.

All well and good, you might say, but what kind of security can come from a God whose power is vulnerable love? The security that God's providence brings is the assurance of provision and the promise of redemption. God draws history to its proper end not by conventional power (that is, control or domination), but by entering the fray of human history and transforming it from within. Jesus reveals to us a God who refuses to make the world turn out right by violently enforcing the good. To do so would be to betray the good by betraying peace. God's ways are not the ways of the world. God is not a "superpower." God does not swoop in to the rescue when things get really bad.

For many the Holocaust stands above all other events as a question mark placed before God. If God did not intervene here, if God did not send angels to end this horror, then how can we trust that God would ever intervene or combat evil directly? Recently, Pope Benedict XVI visited Poland, and while there he journeyed to Auschwitz. "To speak in this place of horror, in this place where unprecedented mass crimes were committed against God and man, is almost impossible—and it is particularly difficult and troubling for a Christian, for a pope from Germany," he said. "In a place like this, words fail. In the end, there can only be a dread silence—a silence which is itself a heartfelt cry to God: Why, Lord, did you remain silent? How could you tolerate all this?"[3] This is the question we all want to ask in the face of suffering and evil. Why would God remain silent? Why would God not intervene? But even the pope confesses that "words fail" when we try to speak of such things. We have no answers that satisfy. We have no answers that do not trivialize or domesticate the suffering. We are left only with silence.

What does such silence mean, in terms of our reflection on divine providence? What does it say about how God does and does not act in the world? In answer to this, we might fruitfully draw on some of Sam Wells's metaphors from theatrical improvisation.[4] In the lingo of improvisation, an actor can

93

respond to an "offer" (an action, speech, or gesture) from another actor by "accepting," "blocking," or "overaccepting." To "accept" is to say yes to the offer and to play out the scene in the terms suggested. To "block" is to say no to the offer. It ends the improvisation by refusing to continue the scene or by rejecting the premise of the offer. Blocking disrupts the scene in such a dramatic way that what follows has no coherence with what preceded. When applied as a metaphor for divine activity, "blocking" is not just God's rejection of our human "offers," but an act that violently or coercively shuts down our capacity to act meaningfully in the world. The flood story in Genesis 6 would constitute an act of blocking, but, of course, God promised after the flood never to "block" the world in this way again. Experiences such as the Holocaust might lead us to conclude that God refuses to "block" the world's actions, even our evil actions.[5]

In contrast, "overaccepting" indicates a willingness to receive the offer, even the evil offer, without blocking, that is, without resisting evil through violence or returning evil for evil. But overaccepting refuses to take the offer on its own destructive terms. Rather, it takes the offer up into a larger frame, a larger narrative, in such a way that the evil offer is overwhelmed by a bigger story and a redemptive hope. Overacceptance could be understood as another description of "transforming fate into destiny." Understood in this way, we might say that Rabbi Michael Goldberg urges "overacceptance" when he suggests that the Holocaust should be interpreted by Jews in light of the bigger and more determinative story of the Exodus.[6] The biblical narrative of God's redeeming Israel from slavery provides a larger context of interpretation in which the Holocaust narratives can be overaccepted, that is, acknowledged in all their horror but not allowed to destroy Jewish faith in the biblical God who ultimately preserves and redeems the people.

In this sense, what my friend Bob did was to overaccept his stroke. He was powerless to block it directly, though he might have sought to block this offer by living the rest of his life in denial, anger, and bitterness. Instead, he overaccepted the offer, he took what happened and reframed it in a bigger story, a story in which God would not let the stroke derail Bob's aspirations. Indeed, the stroke became, in this bigger story, an opportunity to regain focus and faith in his life.

It strikes me that the story of Joseph in Genesis could be read as a story of overaccepting, just as it can be read as a story of providence. When Joseph's brothers attack him and sell him to slave traders, he does not block their actions, either by responding violently to them or by, later, seeking revenge upon them. Rather, he accepts his "fate" but transforms this fate through overacceptance. At the end of the story Joseph narrates, we see his ordeal not only as the work of his brothers but as the work of God. He says to them, "Even though you intended to do harm to me, God intended it for good" (Gen. 50:20). God acts in and through the actions of Joseph's brothers, neither blocking their evil intentions nor simply accepting them and leaving Joseph to die as a slave. God overaccepts the evil offer and thus brings about a good result (when Joseph helps the Egyptians prevent a famine) that would not have happened if God or Joseph had simply blocked the offer.

The cross of Christ would be, perhaps, the most powerful example of God's overaccepting of an evil human offer. Jesus does not block the efforts of Judas or Pilate or the Roman soldiers. He does not become violent, he does not draw upon his secret stock of divine superpower to get him out of this mess. He goes to his death, but he does not let death win. The resurrection is the ultimate theological overaccepting, and this tells us a great deal about how God acts providentially in the world. If God does not use coercive power to block evil and suffering, then we should not expect God to protect us from every harm. Rather, we should seek to align ourselves with the overaccepting God, knowing that God will provide what we need to go on and will redeem what is lost along the way.

I think this is what Jesus meant when he said, "strive first for the kingdom of God and his righteousness, and all these things will be given to you as well" (Matt. 6:33). In the context of the Sermon on the Mount, these words appear as Jesus is talking to his disciples about their fears and insecurities. "Therefore I tell you, do not worry about your life, what you will eat or what you will drink, or about your body, what you will wear" (Matt. 6:25). Why not? Because "your heavenly Father knows that you need all these things" (Matt. 6:32), and they will be added. Jesus reveals that our security, that is, our provision, emerges as a byproduct of seeking God and living the way of the kingdom. To the extent that we seek to secure our own goods apart from participating in the kingdom, we become like the thief who sneaks over the fence into the sheepfold rather than going through the gate. We mistake penultimate things (security) for ultimate things (the reign of God), and so we seek them in the wrong way, indeed, in ways that guarantee we will ultimately lose them. Seek *first* the kingdom of God, we are told. Security cannot be our primary goal. Being safe cannot take precedence over being faithful. And if being faithful makes us unsafe? If being faithful results in suffering? Then we trust that God will provide, God will redeem our losses, God will, in the fifth act of this great drama, reincorporate all things in the heavenly city.[7]

An E-mail Exchange on God, Death, and Providence

Last summer I received an e-mail from a former student, now herself a teacher, telling me the bad news that a friend and student of hers had died.

We exchanged several e-mails in the weeks and months that followed. I include a portion of this exchange here as a way of trying to display what it might look like to draw on a narrative understanding of providence in the context of an actual tragedy, when real people have real questions about God's participation in our world. Hopefully, this exchange gives a window into a moment when all of this reflection on God, providence, suffering, and fear suddenly mattered.

―― Original Message ――
From: Kate Brennan
Date: Friday, July 1, 2005 3:54 am
Subject: Advice

Hey Scott,

So glad I wrote you last week with a positive update of my life. Sadly, within the last week, things have taken a drastic turn, so I figured I would write and appeal to your theological sensibilities.

Since I graduated, I have been teaching private voice lessons in several local schools and have also started my own studio in which I visit students' houses weekly. I tend to get very close with my students and their families and become very much a part of their lives, as they do mine, especially the handful of young women in my own studio. My mother often calls them "the younger sisters I never had" as we are hardly a generation apart. This was very much the way my own vocal teacher worked with me over the past dozen years—often 70% therapist, 30% music instructor.

This past Sunday, I lost one of my students, Ani. She was seventeen and entering her senior year of school. We were particularly close because not only have I been her teacher, but our mothers teach at the same school and often marveled at having such similar daughters, separated by a mere five years.

It's hard to believe I felt Ani's head a bit over a week ago for a fever. By Father's Day, she was in the hospital with inexplicable symptoms—constant fever, unnatural kidney function, failing vision. . . . On Saturday, I got a call that said she had 24 hours left. I was able to visit her at the hospital several times, and hastened to make her an album of the music we worked on because the doctors said that all she responded to was music therapy. . . . When I saw her in the hospital, she was already on a ventilator and unconscious, but I spoke to her anyway.

[Since Ani's death] I've been busying myself along with my Mom in staying with Ani's Mom at her home, organizing food, answering calls, etc. I arranged the music for the services today and sang the entire mass. It was the most difficult thing I've had to do, but Ani must've helped me hold it together throughout the service. Now the funeral and burial are over; I just feel worse with each passing day.

So, naturally, I've been thinking about all of this theological stuff constantly, so I figured I'd write to you. There's no making sense of this loss. Ani emanated an incredibly positive and loving energy and was so talented, I almost feel guilty in having had her sing only for me every week.

I suppose that all those that I've lost have been my own age or older, and never my junior. I don't question or regret any time or action that I took with her; all of my students know how much I care about them and how important they are to me, and Ani must've especially known because our mothers are so close. I praised her and challenged her fittingly and I know that she was a mature, thoughtful, and convivial young woman who lived her short life to the fullest.

Nevertheless, I feel this weight—like a pile of cold wet blankets weighs on my chest and suffocates me more with every breath. I feel as if I walk in a haze and can't really comprehend how people walk around and interact and perform mundane tasks. I realize that these things take time, but I find it difficult to go into houses like hers and teach these other students, unique like her . . . but I know I have a responsibility to them (and her) to continue.

So, I guess I need some theological assurance. How do people cope with so sudden and tragic a loss? How do people find the energy to get up and walk about and drive around and make plans? How do I reassign meaning to these daily things that suddenly seem so pointless? How do I stop resenting others for having fun or placing value on things that I can see now just don't really matter? And how do I find the joy when I feel like someone has literally come in with a vacuum cleaner and sucked the joy out of my life? I've kept myself busy this week until now with plans for Ani, but where the heck can I go from here?

Anyway, I guess it's therapeutic to write. I wrote Maureen, Ani's mom, a letter about Ani and how she touched my life, which I hope provided her with what little solace one can receive at the loss of a child. And it's felt good to write to you; I'm sorry if I have bombarded you with a ton of ponderings.

Thanks in advance for listening. Hope you are well.

~Kate

To: Kate Brennan
From: Scott Bader-Saye
Date: Friday, July 1, 2005 9:32 am
Subject: Re: Advice

Hi Kate,

I'm so sorry to hear about Ani's death. It's always a crushing thing to face an unexpected death, but in one so young it's almost unbearable. I understand the experience you describe of having all the joy and meaning sucked out of everyday things. When something like this happens it seems right that the world would stop, that everyone would pause and take notice, that we would all agree that we can't return to life as usual. The very fact that the world keeps turning seems an affront to the dead and the grieving.

I have thought a lot about God and suffering, and at the very least I've concluded that the banal slogans we sometimes trot out at times like this are usually unhelpful and sometimes harmful. I've heard people, with good intentions I'm sure, say things like "God wanted another angel," or "It was her time." But we all know in our hearts it was not her time—that's the horror of it, that's why we weep uncontrollably at the loss of the young, while the death of the old allows our grief to mix with thanksgiving for a full life. I don't believe God causes disease to take those we love. That's simply not the character of the God I've come to know through the stories of scripture and the life of the church. God is a God of life, not death. What that means, then, is that for some reason God has chosen to allow things to happen that are not God's will. But this does not mean that God leaves us alone in our suffering and grief or that events are purely random.

As I read scripture, and look at my own life, God's usual pattern of working is not to prevent evil and suffering but to provide a way through it and to redeem what is lost. So, although tragedy is real and painful, it is always penultimate in God's story. For Ani the last word is not death but resurrection. God redeems evil by refusing to allow it the last word, by turning even evil to good (which does not mean that Ani's death was in any way good, but that God can bring good even from evil, as Paul tells us in Romans 8:28). It's hard sometimes to accept that good could come, because it may seem to be a betrayal of the dead, as if we could somehow conceptually make their loss "worth it." Certainly not. The good that comes is not a justification of evil or suffering, it does not make it "right" in any way; it is simply God's gift to the broken. I know, for instance, that in a particularly dark time of my life, when I felt that the suffering was unbearable, I had an experience of being "hollowed out" by the pain. This has over time created in me a space that is both emptiness and openness, so that the pain and grief of others can more easily find a place in me.

God's determination to redeem (to "buy back" or reclaim what was lost) gives us hope that in the end God's "Yes" is more powerful than the "No" of evil, suffering, and death. God provides. God redeems. But in many cases, God does not prevent. I sometimes wish it were otherwise and that God were constantly preventing evil, suffering, and death. And it is beyond me to understand how evil has gained a foothold in God's creation (though I know that in some way, small or large, each of us participates in its perpetuation). The story of cross and resurrection tells me that even the best person cannot avoid suffering, even the best life is not immune to tragedy. But, again, tragedy is only act four. Act five is where God reclaims the lost, redeems the evil, restores life and goodness.

In the Episcopal burial service we say at the graveside, "In sure and certain hope of the resurrection to eternal life through our Lord Jesus Christ, we commend to Almighty God our brother/sister." I like these words because they affirm that we believe resurrection to be "sure and certain," but they are honest enough to confess that we hold this conviction as a "hope." My hope for you is that you can find hope. Not just hope in the resurrection for Ani (and ultimately for ourselves as well), but hope that over time your own ability to feel joy, see beauty, enjoy small daily gifts will return. Speaking not just as a theologian but as a person who has known pain, I believe that by some great grace, God always makes it possible for us to again say "yes" to life in a way that no longer seems a betrayal or a forgetfulness of the lost.

I wish you God's peace.
Scott

There would be no need for an e-mail exchange such as this in a world where God protected all the good and faithful people, where we could count on God's providence to mean that we were "secure" in a conventional sense. But that is not the world we live in. God promises to provide. God promises to redeem. God does not promise that nothing bad will ever happen to us. In fact, Jesus promises that if we follow him, the world will persecute us just as it persecuted him. If anything, we are promised suffering, but we are also promised the way through it.

Christian trust in God's providence tells us that if things haven't ended well, then, well, they haven't ended. As Wells has noted, the simple word *and* "constitutes a significant statement. It indicates that the sentence is not yet finished. The story is not yet over. There is more to come, even when evil has done its worst. . . . If one is able to face up to a threat, stare it in the face, and say 'And . . . ?' one has gone a long way toward disarming the threat."[8] This affirmation, along with all the other things we have said about providence in this chapter, may comfort us in times of trouble or even help us make some sense of how God acts in the world.

However, the Christian affirmation of providence ought to do more than this. Providence, first and foremost, names the conditions in which we can, with courage and hope, follow Jesus in a dangerous world. Thus, it ought to shore up our resolve to live the risks of Christian discipleship in a culture of fear. In the next chapters we will explore in more detail the practices made possible by providence.

Questions for Discussion

1. Have you ever wondered about the tension between biblical claims about God's provision, such as, "The Lord will keep you from all evil," and the reality of pain and suffering among good and faithful people? Has this chapter helped you think about that problem in any new ways? Has it resolved any of the tension for you or helped you be able to live with the tension better?

2. Look back at the story of Steve and Dave. What do you think of the woman's view that Steve would be healed of cancer if only he had enough faith? What's wrong with this assumption? Did you find Steve's letter to be a better description of God's provision?

3. Does it make sense for Christians to believe in real contingency, real accidents in this world ("sh-t happens"), while at the same time believing in God's providential care ("God is my co-pilot")? How might we hold these two things together? Why would we want to?

4. Are you convinced by this chapter that God generally does not prevent evil (that is, God does not "block" our evil actions) but that God does provide and redeem ("overaccept")? How does this challenge our usual assumptions about God's "power"? Is this a denial of God's power or a rethinking of that power? How might this affect the way Christians pray?

5. How do you think you would have answered Kate's e-mail before reading this chapter? How might you answer it now? Share ideas of what things we might say to those who are suffering in order to avoid trivializing their pain or resorting to platitudes.

8

The Risk of Hospitality

■ I am convinced that trust in God's providence makes possible the development of the virtues, such as courage, hope, and patience, that are necessary to negotiate a broken and sometimes dangerous world in ways that are expansive, life-giving, and even a bit risky. The assurance that God's purposes for the world (and for each of us) will ultimately be fulfilled makes it possible for us to stop thinking so much about how to be safe and begin thinking more about losing our lives so that we might find them.

In one of my favorite scenes from C. S. Lewis's *The Lion, the Witch, and the Wardrobe,* two young girls, Lucy and Susan, learn from the Beaver family that Aslan, the Christ-figure of the story, is actually a lion.

> "Ooh!" said Susan, "I'd thought he was a man. Is he—quite safe? I shall feel rather nervous about meeting a lion."
>
> "That you will, dearie, and no mistake," said Mrs. Beaver, "if there's anyone who can appear before Aslan without their knees knocking, they're either braver than most or else just silly."
>
> "Then he isn't safe?" said Lucy.
>
> "Safe?" said Mr. Beaver. "Don't you hear what Mrs. Beaver tells you? Who said anything about safe? 'Course he isn't safe. But he's good. He's the King, I tell you."[1]

By choosing to make Aslan a lion (and not, for instance, a lamb) Lewis chose to emphasize the awe-inspiring grandeur of God in a way that resists our inclination to domesticate the divine. Following this kind of God will lead us into the unknown where safety is simply not the point. Like Abraham setting out from Ur, like the Israelites setting out from Egypt, like the disciples following a Messiah who had no place to lay his head, so Christians today follow God not to seek safety, but to participate in a quest for fragile goodness and thereby to find our fulfillment as human beings.

The last three chapters of this book will explore ways that we might live into the risky discipleship made possible when we cease to let fear determine our lives. We will look at three of the Christian practices that are most threatened in a culture of fear: hospitality, peacemaking, and generosity.

Beyond Suspicion

As we noted in chapter 2, the ethic of security produces a skewed moral vision. It suggests that suspicion, preemption, and accumulation are virtues insofar as they help us feel safe. But when seen from a Christian perspective, such "virtues" fail to be true virtues, since they do not orient us to the true good—love of God and neighbor. In fact, they turn us away from the true good, tempting us to love safety more than we love God.

Just to the extent that suspicion comes to be seen as a virtue, hospitality suffers. When the government calls on citizens to watch for suspicious activity in airports, in malls, on the highway, and in any public place, we become trained to see the stranger (or the strange) as threatening. In some cases, even those with different political viewpoints count as "suspicious." Marc Schultz, a bookstore worker in Atlanta, tells the story of being interviewed by the FBI back in 2003 because of an article he was reading in a café. The agent informed Schultz that "someone in the shop that day saw you reading something, and thought it looked suspicious enough to call us about. So that's why we're here, just checking it out." And then, turning on the FBI charm, he added, "Like I said, there's no problem. We'd just like to get to the bottom of this. Now if we can't, then you may have a problem. And you don't want that."[2]

It turns out that Schultz had made the mistake of reading an article entitled, "Weapons of Mass Stupidity," an essay critical of the Bush administration and the news media. Post-9/11 anxiety led someone to believe that this behavior was "suspicious" enough to call the FBI. We do not have to imagine political motives here to be worried by such stories. For while we might find this episode funny (in a way), it indicates a widespread confusion about patriotism and responsibility. To the extent that ordinary citizens come to see the war against terror as their own war, they find suspicion to be an ally in the fight. We dare not trust the stranger when we are at war. And yet we find ourselves in a kind of war that never ends, an eternal war that, if we are not careful, would relegate hospitality to a quaint practice from happier times. Indeed hospitality, especially in a social or a political sense, could come to be seen as irresponsible and morally questionable.

Another example may be helpful here. Not long after 9/11 national security agents thought they picked up the word *Tappahannock* while eavesdropping on suspicious radio transmissions. The people in Tappahannock, Virginia, population 2,068, began wondering whether they would be the next terrorist target. In his documentary *Fahrenheit 9/11,* Michael Moore interviewed some of the townspeople. One woman confessed, "When I look at certain people I wonder, ooh, my goodness, do you think they could be a terrorist?" And when asked, "Do you feel extra suspicious of outsiders?" one auto mechanic responded, "Oh, well, everybody does that. That's just something that happens. . . . Never trust nobody you don't know. And even if you do know them, you really can't trust them then."[3] Distrust becomes a way of life, even in the small town of Tappahannock, where people can only speculate that they might be a terrorist target because of the large Wal-Mart in town. Of course, this is part of the intent of terrorism, to create a climate of fear that poisons ordinary human relations with suspicion. To accept this as a way of life is to give the terrorists a kind of victory. If we are to follow Christ in this kind of atmosphere, it will take a dedicated effort to resist the habit of suspicion and name it as a false virtue.

Community as Threat to Hospitality

Unfortunately, it is not only terrorism that threatens hospitality today. In a climate of fear, the creation of strong communities can produce a lamentable backlash against the outsider. Above, in chapter 5, I suggested that we *need* strong communities to overcome debilitating fear. We need others with whom we can share our fears, pool our resources, and sustain our courage. But the dark side of community shows itself in the strong boundaries we erect to maintain our sense of safety.

A church I was part of for many years liked to speak of itself as a "church family." We knew each other well, we even liked each other, and we spent time together in fellowship outside of Sunday morning. The church members cared for one another in real and tangible ways. Like any good family, we put up with the odd "relative" or two, those who carried a chip on their shoulder and now and again made trouble just to keep us on our toes. We thought of ourselves as "friendly" because we were a "family."

But in practice, friendliness and family don't always go together. What a rude awakening it was to begin to hear from some of the members how inhospitably they were welcomed when they first arrived. Apparently the church members all enjoyed each other's company so much that newcomers were largely ignored. They were welcomed to integrate themselves into the nice family atmosphere we had created, but they needed to take the initiative to get to know us and how we do things. They should not come in with new ideas or expect us to make changes to accommodate their differences. In some ways our closeness as a community made it all the more difficult for us to be open to others. We liked what we had, and we didn't want anyone to come in and mess it up.

Sociologist Zygmunt Bauman has written about the two-edged sword of community, especially in a fearful world where community means security. He observes, "Out there, in the street, all sorts of dangers lie in ambush; we have to be alert when we go out, watch whom we are talking to and who talks to us, be on the look-out every minute. In here, in the community, we can relax—we are safe, there are no dangers looming in dark corners (to be sure, hardly any 'corner' here is 'dark'). In a community, we all understand each other well, we may trust what we hear, we are safe most of the time and hardly ever puzzled or taken aback. We are never strangers to each other."[4] And yet, Bauman notes, this kind of community is an elusive paradise. It is what we want community to be but rarely what it is. Nonetheless, we work hard to approximate this kind of idyllic, peaceful space. But there is a price to be paid, and that price includes the diminishing or extinguishing of hospitality.

Communities, as they really exist, often sustain their unity through their distinctiveness. According to Bauman, "distinctiveness" creates a "division into 'us' and 'them' [that] is exhaustive as much as it is disjunctive, there are no 'betwixt and between' cases left, it is crystal-clear who is 'one of us' and who is not, there is no muddle and no cause for confusion—no cognitive ambiguity, and so no behavioural ambivalence."[5] Community often demands homogeneity, sameness, and clear boundaries as a precondition for that "family" feeling.

In contrast to the secure sameness of the community, Bauman continues, "Strangers are unsafety incarnate and so they embody by proxy that insecurity which haunts your life. In a bizarre yet perverse way their presence is comforting, even reassuring: the diffuse and scattered fears, difficult to pinpoint and name, now have a tangible target to focus on, you know where the dangers reside and you need no longer take the blows of fate placidly. At long last, there is something you can do."[6]

Just as we long for a diagnosis when we are sick, so we long for a way to name and locate our chaotic fears. Once we have a diagnosis, we know how to respond to our illness. We feel that we can *do* something. Likewise, once we locate an object for our fear, we feel empowered. We can now take tangible steps to make ourselves more safe. Insecurity is no longer the sad reality of a fallen and vulnerable world; it is the result of "those" people who pose a tangible and definable threat to "us" and our way of life. Indeed, we exist as "us" precisely because we oppose what "they" are and what "they" do. The cozy feeling of community coexists with an anxious pugnacity that arises, in most communities, as an inevitable byproduct of a shared identity.

These sociological observations about how human communities often work provide a foundation for certain "church growth" programs that exhibit a faux hospitality that ultimately serves to reinforce homogeneity and resist true welcome of the other.[7] For instance, some church growth manuals suggest that churches use demographic information about the areas surrounding the church to target groups who are most likely to fit in and feel welcome in their congregation.[8] Churches will grow most quickly, we are told, if they target a particular demographic. This recipe for a homogeneous community releases churches from the hard work of offering real hospitality to the stranger, since demographic targeting makes sure that none of the newcomers are actually "strange." I do not imagine that these church growth techniques represent ill will toward any particular group; the resulting segregation by race or class is only a byproduct of an efficient marketing strategy. These churches, many of which are desperate for new members to "keep the doors open," are seduced by promises of growth. Yet in a culture of fear these strategies only reproduce a fortress mentality that allows us to feel both safe and welcoming precisely as we exclude the stranger.

As a member of the Evangelism Commission for my diocese, I recently (reluctantly) attended a seminar on church growth. We were taught to gauge the health of a parish in terms of net growth (or loss) in "pledging units" (that's what they call families) and to seek the "lowest cost strategy to reverse numerical decline."[9] All of this corporate language struck me as strangely out of place, since the God of the Bible does not seem to be interested in "cost-effective strategies." Paying workers more than they deserve (see the parable of the laborers in the vineyard, Matt. 20:1–16), calling a small, "stiff-necked" group of people to be his marketing reps (see the covenant with Israel, Deut. 7:7; Exod. 32:9), and unveiling his new product to sheep and horses rather than kings and entrepreneurs (see the birth of Jesus in a stable, Luke 2:1–7) do not look very strategic. Indeed, at the center of God's upside-down kingdom is the reversal of these supposedly prudential judgments about what is effective in the world's eyes. And showing hospitality to the stranger in a fearful world ranks high among God's nonstrategic strategies.

Community as Context for Hospitality

So, is there any way to avoid the inhospitality that forms the dark underside of many communities? Can we have true hospitality in a culture that commends suspicion of the stranger as a patriotic act? Does the Christian tradition have any resources to imagine and embody communal life in ways that do not require exclusion for identity?

Christians have wrestled with these issues since our earliest days, leaving us some helpful guidance as we try to live hospitably in fearful times. First, we may be instructed by the early church council in which the young Christian movement had to make a decision about the inclusion of the Gentiles. Second, we may find wisdom in Paul's description of the church as the body of Christ—one body with many members, one Spirit with many gifts. Finally, we may learn to embody community in the pattern of the three-in-one life of the God who is Trinity.

In the Book of Acts, the early church arises from a fearful band of disciples huddled in an upper room. With the outpouring of the Holy Spirit on Pentecost, this group of followers finds courage to preach and live the way of Jesus. But it is not long before that calling produces a profound challenge to the community. Up until the middle of the Book of Acts, the followers of Jesus are clearly defined as a Jewish group marked by their belief in Jesus as the Messiah of Israel. Increasingly, however, their experience of the Holy Spirit calls into question the boundaries of the community. First, we read in chapter 8 that Philip baptizes an Ethiopian eunuch. As an Ethiopian this man represents the otherness of the sub-Saharan African; as a eunuch he represents someone whose physical state excludes him from Jewish life, even as a convert (Deut. 23:1). Yet without regard for these two strikes against the man, Philip baptizes the Ethiopian into the community of Christ. Next, in Acts 10 we read of Peter taking the good news of Jesus to Cornelius, a Roman centurion. Not only does Peter break Jewish law by lodging and eating with a Gentile, but when Cornelius and his household believe the good news and receive the Holy Spirit, Peter baptizes them. Finally, we read that Paul and Barnabas are received by the Gentiles who believe and follow Jesus, even as their message is rejected by their fellow Jews.

These events lead the church to call its first council in Jerusalem. The meeting is described in Acts 15. The point of contention is whether or not Gentiles have to become Jews first in order to become Christians. This would mean laying the full obligations of Torah on the new believers, including circumcision for the men. Neither Philip nor Peter nor Paul had demanded such full obedience to Torah for the Gentiles they had baptized, and some in the Jerusalem church believed they were thereby unilaterally altering the traditions and disobeying God. What right did these apostles have to release Christians from following Torah? This was not just an issue of behavior, it was an issue of boundaries. Circumcision and food laws were identity markers for the Jews—they showed who was in and who was out. So, the question arose: who could be included in this new community? Could Gentiles *as Gentiles* be received as full members of the church?

On the one side was all the weight of scripture and tradition. God had clearly commanded a separation of Jew and Gentile in Torah. To unite the two in one community would be to ignore God's word. Further, the Jews had for centuries maintained their identity precisely by defining themselves over against the Gentile nations. How could this Jewish movement claim to be in continuity with the past if it ignored God's word and flouted tradition? Peter, in response, tells his story about how God sent the Holy Spirit upon Cornelius and his family, claiming them as followers of Christ. Peter had very little to appeal to beyond his own experience of the Spirit, but he urged his fellow Christians to make permeable the boundaries of the community, to exhibit radical hospitality to those who had for so long been the excluded "other."

In the end, James, the leader of the Jerusalem church, interpreted for the council the words of Amos, "I will return, and I will rebuild the dwelling of David . . . so that all other peoples may seek the Lord—even all the Gentiles over whom my name has been called" (Acts 15:16–17). Instead of reading this as a promise of the conversion of the Gentiles into Jews, James read this passage as a promise to break down the Jew/Gentile distinction. He then decided that the Gentiles should not have to keep Torah and, most significantly at the time, should not have to be circumcised in order to join the church.

This experience in the life of the church gives Christians today a window into the radical hospitality that was necessary for the church to live into its calling in its earliest days. Welcoming the Gentiles was a risky move on all counts, but the willingness of the church to take such a risk provides a paradigm of hospitality for the church today as we face our own temptations to draw sharp boundaries and keep ourselves safe from a hostile world.

Brian McLaren, a pastor and leading figure in the emerging-church conversation, has suggested that we shift our image of church from a "bounded set" to a "centered set."[10] "Bounded sets" are those that are defined by a clear boundary at the edges. You are either in or out of the set. "Centered sets," in contrast, have no clear boundary at the edge but are defined by each member's relation to the center. McLaren suggests that we in the church most properly define ourselves not by the boundaries we create to define who is outside (as in a bounded set) but by our relation to Jesus as our center. The important question then becomes not "Are you in or out?" but "Are you moving toward or away from the center?"

This rethinking of what makes us "us" allows for a fuzzy border when it comes to "belonging" to the group, and it renders obsolete any simple in/out distinction. Of course, this means that we may have to live with a bit more fluidity in our identity. Without sharp boundaries we must be ready to let our identities morph over time, allowing the stranger to become friend and in so doing change in some way how we see ourselves. As Christine Pohl notes, "boundary issues are always slightly ambiguous when we realize that God is already working in the life of every person who comes. Recognizing this opens each community to what God might be saying, what it can learn from the stranger/guest. It keeps the possibility alive that the boundaries could be redrawn."[11]

The identity issue is a hard one, because being hospitable means welcoming people into something, but if you have fuzzy boundaries, do you have a "something" to welcome people into? It seems to me that in order to avoid the dangers of being a community defined by exclusion, we have to be willing to have an identity that is always being discovered, negotiated, reinterpreted, and through Christ ever again received as gift. "Part of the difficulty in recovering hospitality," Pohl writes, "is connected with our uncertainty about community and particular identity. Hosts value their 'place' and are willing to share it; strangers desire welcome into places that contain a rich life of meaning and relationships. By welcoming strangers, however, the community's identity is always being challenged and revised, if only slightly. While this is often enriching, it can occasionally stretch a place beyond recognition."[12]

Benedictine writer Adalbert deVogüé notes that the practice of hospitality is particularly challenging in a monastic context because of this tension between the shared identity of a close-knit community and the porous boundaries needed to allow openings for others. He explains these as two related aspects of following Christ. "Separation and hospitality are therefore two manifestations of the same love: following Christ and receiving Christ. The following draws us out of the world, but there again he comes to us under the appearances of those who are in the world, and we receive him. Then the love which has provoked the separation is verified in hospitality."[13]

Just as the inclusion of the Gentiles meant a radical rethinking of the identity of the early church, so today hospitality to the excluded other will mean opening ourselves to the possibility of learning something new about what it means to follow God in Christ. To the extent that we are unwilling to do this, to the extent that we "welcome" others only insofar as they already reflect who we are, we have not yet begun to embody hospitality.

One Body, Many Members—One God, Three Persons

Hospitality requires that a community be capable of receiving difference as gift. One way of thinking about this kind of community comes from the apostle Paul, who often uses the metaphor of a body to describe the church. This metaphor works so well because the body has a unity that does not destroy difference. Indeed, the body can only function based on the differences of the members. "If the whole body were an eye, where would the hearing be? If the whole body were hearing, where would the sense of smell be? . . . If all were a single member where would be body be? As it is, there are many members, yet one body" (1 Cor. 12:17–20). Understanding the church as the body of Christ allows us to think of it as a place where differences can be reconciled in harmonious action. To the extent that this metaphor actually shapes our communities, Christians have an answer for Bauman's concern that no community can really exist that does not smother true difference. The question is how far we are ready to go to allow real difference to exist in the members of the body and to what extent this difference can be gathered into coordinated work on behalf of Christ.

The body-of-Christ metaphor allows us to imagine unity-in-difference that is not unlike the unity-in-difference of the God who is Trinity. Christians believe that God is one and three, one being in three persons, or one being with three "ways of being." The three "persons" of the Trinity—Father, Son, and Holy Spirit—are different yet the same. I have always been drawn to the Eastern Christian language of *perichoresis* as a description of the Trinity. While we usually translate this Greek term in technical ways like "mutual indwelling," I prefer to look back to the metaphor embedded in the concept. Since "peri-" means "around" (as in "perimeter"), and "-choresis" means "to dance" (as in "choreograph"), I like to imagine the divine life as the "dancing around" of three persons. As with any dance, the three persons must take different but complementary steps in order to keep the dance alive (in a waltz, for instance, my partner had better step back as I step forward, or we're in trouble!). The coordinated motion gains its beauty from the elegant interweaving of difference. Here in the very life of God is the condition of possibility for a difference that does not become competitive, an otherness that does not provoke a struggle for ascendancy. Rather, difference can be held together in a unity of purpose, in an eternal dance of love in which we are all invited to participate.

Hospitality to the stranger, then, enacts not only the church's self-description of a body with many members but the church's description of God as an eternal dance of love. As we welcome the difference of the stranger, we take up the challenge of asking how the dance might be extended to incorporate the new steps this stranger brings to us. Which is to say, Christians, perhaps more than others, should be ready to receive the stranger as gift. Only as the stranger is made friend can we know we are doing the reconciling work we have been given by Christ. And the stranger is not made friend by extinguishing the strangeness but by incorporating his or her difference into an ever more complex dance or, to shift the metaphor, an ever richer harmony.

Saying Yes

A friend of mine, the priest at Trinity Church in Easton, Pennsylvania, recently learned something about the politics of hospitality. About a year and a half ago a young family whose primary language is Spanish began attending worship at his church. In response to their presence, the church community decided to make their worship bulletin bilingual—printing the lessons, prayers, and some announcements in Spanish as well as English. When the family asked to have their baby baptized on Pentecost, the church celebrated with a bilingual liturgy. This small act of hospitality, stretching the community just a bit to accommodate this new family, opened the door to visits and inquiries from other Spanish-speaking families.

What makes this story interesting is that while this church was taking these steps of hospitality, a nearby city in the same diocese gained national attention for its harsh regulations targeting illegal immigrants. Mayor Louis J. Barletta led the city of Hazleton to pass an ordinance that fined landlords $1,000 per day for renting to illegal immigrants, banned businesses that hire illegal immigrants from doing business with the city, and made English the official language of the city. Mayor Barletta was quoted as saying, "They don't belong here. They're not legal citizens and I don't want them here."[14] Though implementation of the legislation has been delayed by court battles, other American cities have been quick to pass similar legislation of their own. For many, the linking of measures targeting "illegals" with the "English-only" ordinance suggests a general antagonism toward the Spanish-speaking community in Hazleton, illegal or not.

In the context of these measures, the small gestures of hospitality at Trinity Church took on political significance. The priest commented, "We have earned a reputation in the community as being a parish that has 'taken a stand' on the current immigration issues, even though our main intent was simply to be pastoral and welcoming to these new families. Of course, this hospitality has guided our parish to go ahead and make the stand, but the two are connected in ways that were surprising to us."[15] What began as an attempt to be faithful to Christ by welcoming the stranger became a witness to the alternative politics of the church.

Theologian David Ford has argued that hospitality may be one of the most important theological virtues for the twenty-first century. He reminds us that hospitality goes beyond a warm welcome and table fellowship (though these are not out of view) to include intellectual hospitality, an openness to hear the story of the other and to receive wisdom from the stranger.

> A theology under the sign of hospitality is formed through its generous welcome to others—theologies, traditions, disciplines, and spheres of life. It has the host's responsibility for homemaking, the hard work of preparation, and the vulnerability of courteously offering something while having little control over its reception. It also has the different responsibility of being a guest, trying to be sensitive to strange households, learning complex codes and risking new food and drink. Ideally, habitual hospitality gives rise to trust and friendship in which new exchanges can plumb the depths of similarity, difference, and suffering.[16]

Ford holds before us the real challenge of hospitality, to welcome the complex otherness of the stranger's traditions and ideas.

Swiss theologian Karl Barth never tired of affirming that God's word to the world in Jesus Christ is not "No" but "Yes." And so we, as followers of Christ, must go forth into the world with that word of yes, knowing that even when we must say no it is in service of a deeper, triumphant yes (perhaps this was Barth's way of talking about "overaccepting"). To be an hospitable people within a culture of fear will require that we learn to say yes when others are quick to say no. It will mean saying yes to the stranger whose language, practices, or worldview strikes us as odd, knowing that underneath any provisional no is a more determinative yes, for the other also bears God's image and might speak truth from unexpected quarters.

Pieces of April: A Parable of Hospitality

I've always thought of the film *Pieces of April* as a wonderful parable of hospitality.[17] The main character, April Burns, is a troubled young woman who has recently moved out of her family's comfortable suburban New York home and taken an apartment in a run-down section of Manhattan.

111

Her relationship with her mother, Joy, has never been good; indeed, Joy comments that she cannot think of one happy memory from April's childhood. As the movie begins we find out that Joy is dying of cancer, that April has invited the family to her apartment for Thanksgiving dinner, and that April cannot cook. The entire movie takes place on Thanksgiving day, beginning in the morning when April discovers, to her dismay, that her oven does not work.

The story revolves around two subplots of hospitality and its absence. The first is April's attempt to welcome her estranged family, and her family's willingness (or unwillingness) to receive that hospitality with grace. The second is April's attempt to find hospitable neighbors who will let her borrow their oven. As she walks door to door in her apartment building, she finds few neighbors willing even to listen to her request. Finally, she knocks on the door of an African-American couple in apartment 2B. The wife, Evette, answers the door. "I have a problem," April tells her. Evette yells in to her husband, "It's the new girl in 3C, says she's got a problem." "What?" he asks. "Problems, Eugene, the girl's got problems. She's white, she's got her youth, her whole privileged life ahead of her. I am looking forward to hearing about her problems." Evette laughs and we recognize the ways that race and class make a hospitable welcome unlikely.

But the scene cuts from Evette's laughter to her tears as she sits on her couch and hears of April's plight. Hospitality involves discovering the humanness of the other, which sometimes just means giving someone the opportunity to tell her story. In the telling, April becomes more than the privileged white girl. She is a daughter whose mother is dying. Evette agrees to put off cooking her turkey for a few hours so that April can get started and buy some time to find another oven. As the turkey cooks, Evette and Eugene offer another kind of hospitality by teaching April some things about cooking (like don't use store-bought stuffing or cranberry sauce out of a can), so that she, in turn, can welcome her family with a proper feast.

After much searching, April finds Wayne in 5D, who will let her use his oven to finish her turkey. But we come to find that Wayne wants something in return for his offer, and when April shows disinterest in him he chides her, "Do you know that good feeling that often comes from being helpful?" "Yes." "I'm not having that feeling here. So I ask myself, 'Wayne, it's very clear what you're doing for her, but what are you getting out of this?' I think you need to take some time and think about that so that maybe later you'll help me understand what I'm getting from this exchange." Unable to show hospitality, Wayne can only construe what is happening as an exchange, turning a neighbor's need into an opportunity for gain. He briefly takes April's turkey hostage but finally releases it (sans a leg pilfered for his cat!).

While April sits forlorn on the apartment steps, a Chinese man approaches and, despite his speaking no English, gestures for her to use his oven. She follows him into the apartment and hears the daughter, the only one who speaks English, say, "Welcome to our home." As the turkey cooks, April tries to explain to this immigrant family the meaning of Thanksgiving.

> Once there were people here called Indians, Native Americans, whatever. And then a boat came called the Mayflower, landed on a big rock, carrying people just like me. And the first year on their own was hard. It was really, really hard. . . . Let me start again. This was long ago, before we stole most of their land, killed most of them, and moved the rest to reservations. Before they lost their language and their customs. . . . Okay. Um. Forget what I just said. Once there was this one day where everybody seemed to know they needed each other. This one day when they knew for certain that they couldn't do it alone.

In her attempts to describe the meaning of Thanksgiving, April catches up the themes of the film—her own struggle to make it on her own, the inhospitable encounter that produces animosity and destruction, and the possibility of hospitality that comes through the recognition that we need each other.

When April's family finally arrives, they are greeted on the street by her African-American boyfriend, whose lip is bleeding from a fight. Looking from him to the run-down apartment building, they abandon their plans and drive off to a diner.

At this point the film begins to parallel quite closely a parable Jesus told about a great dinner:

> Someone gave a great dinner and invited many. At the time for the dinner he sent his slave to say to those who had been invited, 'Come; for everything is ready now.' But they all alike began to make excuses. . . . So the slave returned and reported this to his master. Then the owner of the house became angry and said to his slave, "Go out at once into the streets and lanes of the town and bring in the poor, the crippled, the blind, and the lame." And the slave said, "Sir, what you ordered has been done, and there is still room." Then the master said to the slave, "Go out into the road and lanes, and compel people to come in so that my house may be filled. For I tell you, none of those who were invited will taste my dinner." (Luke 14:16–21)

A dinner that began as an offering to those who might return hospitality becomes a meal given freely to those who cannot repay. This kind of radical hospitality, Jesus tells us, is a sign of the reign of God.

Pieces of April narrates just such a sign in its closing minutes. April, having lost her invited dinner guests, invites her Chinese neighbors to share the feast. Her family's rejection of the meal created a space for a hospitable welcome of the stranger. While this is going on, April's mother decides to return to April's apartment; she walks out of the diner and hitches a ride with a stranger on a motorcycle. As the film ends, April's mother arrives for the meal, which now includes not only the Chinese family and the invited guests, but the motorcycle rider, Evette from 2B, and finally the rest of her family.

The table overflows with hospitality that has been extended well beyond the expected guests. Unlike the parable, those who were invited *do* taste the dinner, but only in the company of all those who now share the meal that had been rejected. This is the unexpected gift of hospitality, not the calculated exchange demanded by Wayne in 5D, but the overflowing of blessing that cannot be predicted.

Eli's Story: Responding to 9/11

For many of us in the United States, the events of 9/11 threatened our ability to extend hospitality. The attacks prompted a kind of recoiling into self, family, and community. Understandably, we sought security in the familiar. My wife and I, however, felt 9/11 as a call to action, a call to reach out to those in need, a call to stretch ourselves. In response to this prompting of the Spirit, we decided to welcome a child into our home through a foster-adopt program. We were not consciously trying to make a statement about welcoming the stranger, for in many ways even our biological children come to us as strangers. But our decision to welcome Eli at that time, in that context, signified for us a decision not to constrict our lives, not to settle back into the safe and the familiar, not to let fear keep us from taking the risk of welcoming Christ in this child. After several years of fostering, we were able to adopt Eli, to claim him as our own. The adoption day was a joyful celebration, not so much of our hospitality, but of God's offering this child to us with all of his unexpected gifts that continue to surprise us and bring us joy.

This is not to say that we have been immune to the fears involved in fostering and adoption. But we have refused to let fear direct our course. We have found through this experience that Pohl's words ring true, "Over and over again, I've come to see that in God's remarkable economy, as we make room for hospitality, more room becomes available to us for life, hope, and grace."[18] In God's abundance, hospitality does not drain us of what we have but adds to our resources. "There is a mutual blessing in hospitality; practitioners consistently comment that they receive more than they give."[19] I remember vividly the mixture of joy and apprehension the day we said yes to Eli, the day we received him as a three-day-old baby in the hospital, a stranger who was destined to become family. His life with us reminds us daily of the God who is not safe but is surely good.

Questions for Discussion

1. What do you think of the idea that God is good but not safe? Does this help you think about God in new and helpful ways, or is the idea troubling? Why?
2. Do you think suspicion makes you less likely to be hospitable to strangers? How do we find the proper balance between being safe and being hospitable? How does this relate to our discussion of courage in chapter 6?
3. Have you ever been part of a church (or visited a church) that was so tight-knit it was hard for new people to break in? Why do churches have a tendency to become cliques? What can be done about it?
4. Think about the tension between identity and hospitality. To what extent does the identity of church (or other groups you might be a part of) rely on who is excluded? Is there a way to have strong identity and extend hospitality at the same time? What would that look like in practice? Do you find the distinction between "bounded set" and "centered set" helpful in this?
5. How does the story of the Jerusalem Council in Acts 15 help us think about issues of inclusion and exclusion today? Does it suggest any tools for how to balance the integrity of the community with an openness to the stranger?
6. Does Paul's analogy of the church as a body or the church's description of God as "three and one" help us describe the balance of unity and difference, identity and hospitality, that we are striving for?
7. At the end of the chapter, I share a fictional story and a real-life story that display something of what hospitality might look like in today's world. Can you think of any stories of hospitality, fictional or real-life, that do the same for you?

9

The Risk of Peacemaking

■ One afternoon, while walking around the Yale campus in New Haven (getting an early start on those college visits!), our six-year-old son Nolan spotted a group of people carrying signs that said, "Stop the War in Iraq" and "Bring the Soldiers Home." Nolan was aware that there was a war going on, but he wanted to know more about why these people were carrying signs. We told him that some people thought we should not have attacked Iraq and that the war was unjust. These people often protested as a way of voicing their concerns about the actions of the government. There was a period of silence, and then Nolan responded by telling us a story from a book he had been reading. The book was *Summer of the Sea Serpent* in the *Magic Tree House* series for children. He recounted a scene from this book and then told us that when he got home he wanted to hand out flyers with excerpts from the story. The next day, when we returned home, he had not forgotten his resolve. He went straight to the computer and began to type his flyer.

The main characters in the story are Jack and Annie, two children from Frog Creek, Pennsylvania, who travel across time and space in a magic tree house. In this volume they encounter a sea serpent guarding an ancient sword. To gain access to the magical sword they must answer the serpent's question, "What is the purpose of the sword?" Jack and Annie quickly try to come up with the right answer—"To defeat your enemies?" "To force them to give up?"—but neither answer rings true.

Jack then remembers the instruction given to the children by Merlin when they began their mission: *"Answer a question with love, not fear."* Jack faces the serpent and his fear fades away. "'The sword should not be used to harm anyone or anything!' Jack shouted. . . . 'The sword should not make people afraid! . . . It should help take away their fear! If they're not afraid, they'll stop fighting! The purpose of the sword is not fighting! The purpose of the sword is *peace!*'"[1] Nolan rightly understood that the wisdom of this children's book had implications for real-world politics. Without even knowing that the Iraq War began as a fearful response to the 9/11 attacks, he assumed that handing out flyers about overcoming fear as a path to peace just might make a difference.

In this chapter we will ask the question, "How can we risk being peacemakers in a fearful world?" If fear naturally orients us toward a violent response, how do we sufficiently overcome fear to live the peace of Christ? For Christians, peacemaking is not an optional side dish in God's great feast. It is at the heart of Jesus's reconciling work. Jesus blesses the peacemakers, saying that they will be called children of God; Jesus tells his followers to turn the other cheek, to love enemies, to bless those who persecute them. Jesus himself refuses to allow his disciples to defend him violently, and he forgives his executioners.

Believing that Christians are called to be peacemakers does not necessarily mean that one must be a pacifist, but it does mean that one always begins with a presumption for peace and a very limited set of circumstances in which that presumption can be overruled by a tragic and just use of force. At its 75th General Convention, during the summer of 2006, the Episcopal Church passed a resolution calling for an end to the war in Iraq. The resolution included this explanation: "We certainly recognize that faithful Christians of good will may disagree with one another when it comes to questions of national policy. We trust, however, that all Christians will pray and work for peace, remembering the words, 'Blessed are the peacemakers, for they will be called children of God.'"[2] Walking in peace and practicing peacemaking are callings for all Christians, pacifists and "just war" Christians alike. Yet the way of peace is deeply threatened by the culture of fear.

Beyond Preemption

Some of us who live in a culture of fear have become predisposed to take preemptive action for the sake of security. Indeed we have come to treat preemption as a virtue. As we noted in chapter 2, fear usually leads us to attack or contract. Thus, preemption can take two forms. Some of us preemptively contract by voluntarily pulling back from uncertain engagements that pose even a slight risk. In so doing we maximize security even as we diminish our exploration of life's mysteries and gifts. We praise ourselves for our wise self-limitation, though this ends up looking a lot like cowardice. Others of us preemptively attack, seeking to destroy the source of our fear or to cause it to contract in the face of our threat. We are willing (some would say required) to strike first if it means we will become safer. We are tempted to believe that if we make others afraid of us, we will not have to be afraid of them.

According to Mark's Gospel, Jesus himself faced the consequences of a fear-based preemptive strike. Mark tells us that the chief priests and scribes wanted to kill Jesus, because "they were afraid of him" (Mark 11:18). Unreflective fear often morphs into anger, and anger sometimes rises to violence, which is meant to end the fear. But, most often, violence simply elicits counterviolence, which produces more fear, and which, if unchecked, spirals into a cycle of retribution. Part of what is remarkable about Jesus's response to those who would kill him out of fear is his refusal to answer violence with violence. Jesus did not let his fear of death provoke him to "preempt" the cross (not that the disciples didn't try, but Jesus told them to put away the sword—Matt. 26:52). Learning to face our fears, to share them in community, and to situate them within a story of God's enduring and unfailing purposes can give us strength to break the cycle, that is, to answer with love, not fear.

In the period after the U.S. invasion of Afghanistan and during the buildup to the invasion of Iraq, a group of Benedictine monks put out a statement about U.S. war policy. They wrote, "One of the main reasons given by the administration for going to war is that, as Americans, we must refuse to live in fear. As people of faith, we know that fear is a spiritual problem. Fear can only be overcome by confronting fear itself, not by eradicating every new object of fear. The answer to fear is not war, but a deep and living faith."[3] These Benedictines recognized the failure of preemption, not just because it fails to meet just-war standards of "last resort" and "just cause," but because preemption falsely assumes that we can overcome fear by destroying every possible threat. Such a project is, in principle, interminable. In a fallen world anyone or anything could become a threat. There is no end to preemption, which is why there should be no beginning.

Providence as Threat to Peacemaking

I have suggested that one of the resources Christians have for overcoming fear is our trust in the providence of God—not a naïve trust that nothing bad will ever happen to us, but a trust that in difficult times God

119

will provide what we need and redeem what is lost. These assurances of providence can go a long way toward relieving us of debilitating fear and helping us live joyfully and peacefully. But providence has often been misused and manipulated to give divine sanction to acts of aggression and oppression.

Douglas John Hall argues that the biblical understanding of providence was distorted by a "theology of glory" intended to support and defend the triumph of Christianity socially and politically in the West.

> What has happened to the biblical testimony to divine providence all too typically in Christian doctrinal history is that it has been subjected to what Luther named *theologia gloriae*—that is, religious triumphalism. An imperial religion could not live with a God whose governance of the world is shrouded in paradox and mystery. An established religion, the official cult of the official culture, had regularly to explain and to vindicate its deity and, in the process, itself. This triumphant providentialism Christendom both learned from and bequeathed to the successive empires with which it cohabited. And none of these empires learned the lessons of this providentialism more impressively than did our own North American imperium.[4]

While a long story could be told of the history of using providence as a political tool, what is significant for us is the way in which this kind of appeal to providence turns the doctrine on its head. Instead of creating a peaceful patience that trusts the future to God's hands, it produces justifications for violent domination.

The problem is that political appeals to providence often function as a divine rubber stamp for human ideologies and interests. When Rome extended its empire by conquering a neighboring state, this was read as a sign of divine providence. When England and Spain colonized the New World, this was taken as a sign of divine providence. When the United States extended its borders and its influence over other people and nations, this was taken as a sign of divine providence.

But if whatever happens is God's will, then whoever wins is God's winner. This distorted use of providence would tell us that if a nation succeeds in dominating others, it is because God wants it to dominate others. Too often, the winners get to write not only the histories but also the theologies. Those who invoke providence to support self-interested aggression never seem too concerned that this puts God on the side of the strong, the rich, and the powerful—the empires of the world—even though Jesus's own life and witness puts God on the side of the poor, the powerless, and the oppressed—the losers of history. Something has gone wrong when we appeal to providence as a theological justification for imperial aggression when God in Christ resisted such powers to the point of death.

Manifest Destiny and the War on Terror

To understand how providence has been misused politically, we would do well to look back to the nineteenth century. Though many European nations were claiming divine sanction for their imperial interests, the United States emerged as the nation most committed to the mythology of a divine mandate. We even produced our own description of this mandate: "manifest destiny." This term was coined by John L. O'Sullivan in an editorial for the *New York Morning News* on December 27, 1845. Urging the westward expansion of America, O'Sullivan argued for "the right of our manifest destiny to over spread and to possess the whole of the continent which Providence has given us."[5] This justification for expansion was widely accepted among the American people, though there were dissenting voices. Note, for instance, the concern expressed in this letter to Senator Henry Clay, written by the Rev. William E. Channing in 1837: "There is no fate to justify rapacious nations, any more than to justify gamblers and robbers, in plunder. . . . We talk of accomplishing our destiny. So did the late conqueror of Europe (Napoleon); and destiny consigned him to a lonely rock in the ocean, the prey of ambition which destroyed no peace but his own."[6] Despite such minority voices, the belief that America was a "chosen nation" with a special calling made the doctrine of manifest destiny seem almost self-evident to many Americans at the time.

As the nineteenth century passed into the twentieth, American providentialism continued to guide public and political rhetoric surrounding expansion. Senator Albert J. Beveridge famously argued that the United States should not stop expanding at the Pacific Ocean but should extend its reach across the ocean to the Philippines. On January 9, 1900, he argued on the Senate floor that America had a "duty" to annex the Philippines. "We will not renounce our part in the mission of our race, trustee under God, of the civilization of the world. The Pacific is our ocean."[7] And as a kind of added bonus, he noted, there just happen to be unlimited economic opportunities in China.[8] For Beveridge this was all understood as part of a divine plan for the privileging of America. "Wonderfully has God guided us Yonder at Bunker Hill and Yorktown. His providence was above us at New Orleans and on ensanguined seas His hand sustained us. . . . The American people can not . . . fly from our world duties; it is ours to execute the purpose of a fate that has driven us to be greater than our small intentions. We can not retreat from any soil where Providence has unfurled our banner; it is ours to save that soil for liberty and civilization."[9]

Lest we think such language is outdated and discredited, we should listen to the language of George W. Bush as he defended the U.S. invasion of Iraq. Though the invocation of providence has been muted, it is still present. Interestingly, the providential appeals shifted significantly from the time before the war began to the time after. In his 2003 State of the Union address, in which he laid out his case for attacking Iraq, Bush ended with these words:

> We Americans have faith in ourselves, but not in ourselves alone. We do not know—we do not claim to know all the ways of Providence, yet we can trust in them, placing our confidence in the loving God behind all of life, and all of history. May He guide us now. And may God continue to bless the United States of America.[10]

While appealing to divine providence Bush shows reticence in claiming that this providence is "manifest" or clearly visible. Bush expresses a confidence in God's providence without necessarily claiming that God has weighed in on the upcoming invasion. "We do not know—we do not claim to know," Bush emphasizes, capturing—rightly, I think—the mystery of God's providence. But note how the tone changes in the 2004 State of the Union address. Again, in his closing words Bush appeals to the divine:

> My fellow citizens, we now move forward, with confidence and faith. Our nation is strong and steadfast. The cause we serve is right, because it is the cause of all mankind. The momentum of freedom in our world is unmistakable—and it is not carried forward by our power alone. We can trust in that greater power who guides the unfolding of the years. And in all that is to come, we can know that his purposes are just and true. May God continue to bless America.[11]

At this point the war in Iraq had been going on for almost ten months, and Bush was willing to identify his war efforts with divine providence. None of the reticence or humility of the 2003 speech remains. Bush's "cause" is right because it is the cause of God, the "greater power who guides the unfolding years." As with O'Sullivan and Beveridge, Bush paints a picture of inevitability, of destiny. America's war effort serves "the momentum of freedom" in the world that is "not carried forward by our power alone" but by the power of God, whose "purposes are just and true." This war effort, then, by implication, must also be just and true.

Appeals to providence can all too easily become justifications for our own self- or national interest. We engage in acts of violence in the name of a god who is conceived of not as Father, Son, and Holy Spirit but as "that greater power." God becomes indistinguishable from some predetermined cosmic fate. But Christianly speaking, God is never that. God's power is never generic or undefined power. It is the power revealed to us in Jesus Christ, this power and no other. Once one begins to think of God in distinctly Christian ways, linking the sovereignty of God to the witness of Christ, it becomes much more difficult to justify domination in the name of providence. For the revealing of God's power in Christ transformed the way we think about power. If we trust that Christ reveals the truth about God, then we must assume that God does not wield power to dominate, coerce, or destroy (since Jesus did not do these things). Thus, God's providential will for the world cannot be read off of the triumph of regimes that dominate, coerce, or destroy.

In a culture of fear we must take great care not to assume that our attempts to become invulnerable to threat are necessarily consistent with God's purposes. In fact, as I will argue below, divine providence, rightly understood, teaches us to trust in God's future so that we may release our desire for control. This kind of trust makes peacemaking possible precisely because we do not have to force God's future (or ours) upon the world.

Providence, Peace, and *Murder in the Cathedral*

The Book of James in the New Testament links conflict and violence to our failure to trust God for our needs. James writes, "Those conflicts and disputes among you, where do they come from? Do they not come from your cravings that are at war within you? You want something and do not have it; so you commit murder. And you covet something and cannot obtain it; so you engage in disputes and conflicts" (James 4:1–2). What is the alternative? James goes on, "You do not have, because you do not ask. You ask and do not receive, because you ask wrongly, in order to spend what you get on your pleasures" (James 4:2–3). James suggests that our violence toward others is the result of a war within ourselves. We attack others because we sense that we do not have what we need, and this is magnified when we confuse our needs with our wants. Violence and covetousness walk hand in hand. James tells us that the solution to our violence comes from our reliance on God's care ("You do not have because you do not ask"). Violence results from a failure to trust God's providence, but when we believe that God will give us what we need, we can let go of our violent attempts to secure what we want.

T. S. Eliot explores the connection between providence and peace in his play *Murder in the Cathedral,* a story about the twelfth-century martyrdom of Thomas Becket, Archbishop of Canterbury, by King Henry II. As the play begins, Becket is returning from exile in France, where he had fled to avoid the threats of the king. Unwilling to yield control of the church to Henry, Becket decides to return to England and stand up to the throne. The play makes clear that Thomas has come to a point where he trusts his fate to God, knowing that even if he dies, it will serve God's cause.

As the soldiers come to kill him, some of his priests bar the doors to the cathedral. Thomas refuses to defend his life by force and commands:

> Unbar the doors! throw open the doors!
> I will not have the house of prayer, the church of Christ,
> The sanctuary, turned into a fortress.
> The Church shall protect her own, in her own way, not
> As oak and stone; stone and oak decay,
> Give no stay, but the Church shall endure.
> The church shall be open, even to our enemies. Open the door![12]

The doors are opened and Thomas is murdered. For Thomas it is more important for the church to maintain its mission as a sanctuary for all people, even enemies, than it is to save his own life.

Eliot identifies Thomas's trust in providence as the key to his courage. This is what allows him to avoid the anxiety that has driven his priests to withdraw and contract and lock the doors on his behalf. Just before his death, Thomas speaks to the women of Canterbury, who are already lamenting his loss:

> Peace, and be at peace with your thoughts and visions.
> These things had to come to you and you to accept them.
> This is your share of the eternal burden,
> The perpetual glory. This is one moment,
> But know that another
> Shall pierce you with a sudden painful joy
> When the figure of God's purpose is made complete.[13]

Thomas knows that in some way his martyrdom will be gathered up into God's purpose, made part of God's great "figuring" of history. Only moments after this, Thomas assures his fellow priests,

> I have had a tremour of bliss, a wind of heaven, a whisper,
> And I would no longer be denied; all things
> Proceed to a joyful consummation.[14]

Here, Eliot echoes a theme from the mystical writer Julian of Norwich, a theme to which he will return several times in his later poetry, most notably in the closing movements of "Little Gidding," the last of the *Four Quartets*. There he writes (quoting Julian), "All shall be well and / All manner of thing shall be well."[15] Eliot places in the mouth of Thomas his own conviction that God's good and joyful purposes will finally be made complete. It is this conviction, this hope, this trust that allows Thomas to let go of the fear of losing his life.

The nonviolence of the martyr witnesses to God's providence. When we trust that "the figure of God's purpose" will be made complete and that "all things proceed to a joyful consummation," we are empowered to overcome our fear of the future. Because we trust God's provision, we need not kill in order to feel safe. We need not make the church or the home a "fortress" against evil. Rather, we can learn to walk confidently in the steps of Thomas, not, for most of us, going to martyrdom, but simply living in the peaceful way of Christ that does not require violence to make us feel safe.

Young Peacemakers

On May 21, 1998, fifteen-year-old Kipland Kinkel carried a gun into Thurston High School in Springfield, Oregon, and shot twenty-three people, killing two. Later it was discovered that he had killed his parents and stockpiled his house with homemade bombs. On the Sunday following this tragedy, Scott Clark, pastor of a church in the area, asked the congregation to pray about how God could use them to help prevent further violence.[16] The people of this church had just finished offering a Young Peacemakers class the previous Sunday. They had planned to offer the class again in a few years but decided that the particular gift their congregation could offer to their broken and hurting community was this program of peace-making for youth. They immediately began to plan for multiple classes to be offered at several locations throughout their area. Almost a quarter of the congregation signed up to participate in this endeavor.

Sue Scott describes their efforts: "We offered classes in Springfield and at our church in a neighboring community, Eugene. Parents were encouraged to attend with children. We decided to hold classes even if one family came because we knew God would bring whoever needed to be there. Classes were free and open to all. It was a community activity; however, we agreed to fully incorporate our religious beliefs. A mere two and a half weeks after the tragedy, we began with four families in each class. The response was very positive."[17] One parent, who attended with her ten-year-old son, commented, "What I liked most about the class was that I now see him thinking before he acts. He isn't as self-centered and is more empathetic."[18] Building on the success of this series of classes, the congregation started another class at a local high school.

In many ways this project was a small gesture in the face of a large problem. Yet for this modest congregation it was, as Scott says, an "ambitious project." In fact, the size of the project required that church to partner with other churches and schools in the community. And that turned out to be one of the gifts of the program. "We believe it will be a powerful testimony to see different congregations working peacefully together."[19] In a culture of fear, where threats are real even when they are unlikely, the witness of churches such as this one helps us imagine faithful and peaceful responses to the things that threaten us. Even when the evil we fear comes to pass, the church need not give up its work for peace, its hope that the witness of Christ can make a difference for the future.

Pacifism and Just War

For many, the issue of war is the most difficult problem for Christian peacemaking. Do we have a duty to support the state and its military? Is peacemaking a concern only for Christian pacifists? I would suggest that both traditional Christian responses to war—pacifism and just war—rely on our trust in God's providence to free us from the fear that would make us use violence in unjust and unfaithful ways.

Christian pacifism rests not on a naïve belief that if we would only lay down our arms, the other side would do the same. It does not deny that sin has distorted the world; it does not presume that the enemy will be moved by our gestures of peace. It does not suppose that we can always reach a peaceful solution through diplomatic channels. It does not deny that in the face of genocide peaceful diplomacy may only provide time for the aggressors to carry out their evil plan. Christians do not become pacifists because they believe it will "work" better. In fact, it will likely make the world more violent, because in some instances it is only the threat of violence that holds violence in check.

The only reason for a Christian to be a pacifist is that one truly believes that God has made peace *with* the world in Christ and that God is making peace *in* the world through our faithful nonviolence. Only if God is actively guiding the world to its harmonious end can Christians risk imitating the nonviolence of Jesus. The point of renouncing violence, then, is not as a strategy for peace but as a witness to the world of the peace that is coming. Christian pacifists so trust that "all will be well" that they can risk renouncing violent means in this the fourth, but not final, act of God's drama. If we can trust the future to God's hands, then we can begin now to live the peace that is coming, and in so doing we can show the world that violence is not inevitable. In Christ, God has made a path for peace, and Christians are those who have been called to walk it without fear, precisely because we know that the fifth act has already been written, the redemption has already happened, and all that is left is to live it.

In a similar way Christian just-war practice rests on a strong conviction about God's providential care for the world. "Just war" names a tradition of discernment in the church in which certain criteria have to be met in order to wage war, and certain limitations are placed on how that war is waged; in short, a nation must go to war for just reasons and wage war in just ways. As Daniel Bell Jr. has pointed out, the Christian practice of just war is quite different from a governmental just-war "checklist." For Christians just war is a form of discipleship, a way of following God in the face of violent threat. Just war requires discipline because the extremity of the situation does not allow us simply to set aside all the virtues by which we follow Jesus on a daily basis—virtues such as faith, hope, love, patience, courage, and wisdom. Engaging in a just war arises as a tragic exception to the presumption for peace but an exception that does not render Christian identity irrelevant to the waging of war.

This takes us back to issue of fear. If we allow fear to overwhelm us, we will not be able to be faithful either as pacifists or as just-war Christians. Fearful pacifists will be tempted to fight, and fearful just warriors will be tempted to fight unjustly. Inordinate fear has a way of convincing us that effectiveness is more important than faithfulness. So, if we think something will be effective in making us more secure, fear prompts us to do it, even if it runs against the teaching of our faith. The need to put fear in its place, then, is just as important for a just-war Christian as for a pacifist. As Bell puts it,

> the call to risk ourselves for others challenges us to confront the pervasive sense of fear and inordinate concern for security that threatens to envelop us. This criterion reminds us of the importance of proclaiming the gospel—that Christ has defeated sin and death, that we need not be consumed by fear, that there are worse things than dying, that we are free to live in holy insecurity, free even to die in service to our neighbor. A people who lack courage in the face of death, whether on neighborhood streets or in the hospital bed, will be hard pressed to resist the temptation to abandon the neighbor or to discard the just war discipline, say, by engaging in preventative strikes against an uncertain threat.[20]

The criteria for just war have been interpreted more or less rigorously at different times by different people. What has always been true, however, is that both just-war and pacifist Christians agree that there are limits on what we can do as followers of Jesus in the face of a violent threat. They define those limits differently, but both agree that Christians are not free to engage in unjust actions, even if those actions are intended for a good purpose. Christian soldiers exhibit true courage in their willingness to risk death rather than preserve their lives through unjust means. Fear, however, tempts us to ignore all restrictions on warfare in order to ensure survival at all costs.

A people who fear death will be hard pressed to sustain just war as discipleship—for it may require facing death on behalf of our neighbor (both the victim and enemy), when fighting unjustly may offer the appearance of avoiding death. The opportunity is to recover the courage of faith, the gift of living in holy insecurity. Then we will be able to take up the cross, serving our neighbors (including our enemies) fearlessly in pursuit of a just peace.[21]

I would add that there is nothing wrong with fearing death to some extent. As we noted in chapter 3, Thomas Aquinas argued that Christians are right to fear death, since it does involve a very real loss of earthly loves. These loves are not to be taken lightly, even if we believe that after death we will be resurrected to eternal life. The problem comes not when we fear death (courage is only real courage if we feel fear), but when we fear it inordinately, fearing it so much that in order to preserve our safety we refrain from doing the good.

Christian just war, as much as pacifism, requires a disciplined life, a readiness to risk self for others, and a willingness to live with insecurity rather than to secure oneself, one's family, or one's nation unjustly. Fear tells us that "all is fair in love and war." But for Christians there can be no such belief. Although war may seem to be the triumph of chaos and thus without rules or parameters, the just-war tradition refuses to believe that in war everything is allowed. For Christians, even war can be waged only within clear boundaries that must be drawn by faith, not fear.

Fear, Patience, and Peace

The just-war criteria are meant to slow down the rush to war, to create a period of dialogue and reflection. Only in this way will we be sure that we are not fighting as a fearful, knee-jerk reaction to danger. But this is no easy task, since fear teaches us to see time as a threat. Every moment seems to lead us closer to dangerous possibilities. "It's just a matter of time before it happens to you," is the message fear sends us—just a matter of time before the terrorists strike again, just a matter of time before you get cancer, just a matter of time before you lose a loved one, just a matter of time before your friends realize you aren't cool, just a matter of time before your "performance" in bed isn't what it used to be (thanks, Bob Dole). As we saw in chapter 1, marketers routinely exploit this fear to sell us their new security/fashion/personal improvement product. When we are afraid, time is not on our side.

Jérôme Bindé makes the case that our current fearfulness tempts us to live perpetually in what he calls "Emergency Time." He describes it this way, "By giving precedence to the logic of 'just in time' at the expense of any forward looking deliberation, within a context of ever faster technological transformation and exchange, our era is opening the way for the tyranny of emergency. Emergency is a direct means of response which leaves no time for either analysis, forecasting, or prevention. It is an immediate protective reflex rather than a sober quest for long-term solutions."[22] Bindé helps us see how living in fear, that is, in a state of emergency, produces an impatience, an unwillingness to deliberate about long-term solutions. We feel that we just don't have time for that. The events of 9/11 threw the United States into a state of panic. We shifted into "emergency time," fearing that another attack might be imminent. But even years later we don't know how to shift out of emergency time, since we are engaged in an ongoing war on terror that seems to have no end. We seem to be stuck in the "immediate protective reflex" that kicked in on 9/11. We imagine that we don't have time for "analysis, forecasting, and prevention," so we turn to the quick, but hardly nuanced, response of force and violence.

All this is to say that fearfulness produces impatience because we fear that we do not have time to discern options other than a profound and immediate show of force ("shock and awe," as George W. Bush put it). One of the gifts of courage is the ability to be patient because we refuse to let fear push us to act before we are ready, that is, before we have taken time to gather the wisdom necessary to judge a situation with prudence. Because Christians trust in God's providence, we believe that time is on our side, that history unfailingly moves toward that fifth act in which God will gather up all things in Christ. Patience, then, as an outworking of our trust in providence, becomes a partner of peace.

Patience is required of pacifism, since the way of nonviolence demands the patient waiting upon God's action to bring the world to its ultimate reconciliation. Patience is also required of just war, since we cannot allow the quick obliteration of the enemy through indiscriminate killing. Yet, as Bell notes, "a culture that teaches instant gratification, that can make little sense of the patient endurance of hardship, that cannot sustain fidelity cannot sustain just war, which requires fidelity to principle and the endurance of much (even defeat!) in the name of those principles."[23]

False Patience

Having encouraged patience as an important Christian virtue, we must be careful not to confuse true patience with false patience. True patience arises from trust in God's future and moves toward justice and peace, while false patience arises from fear and supports the status quo. During the civil rights struggle of the 1960s, Martin Luther King Jr. wrote a letter from the Birmingham jail addressed to eight white religious leaders in Alabama. These leaders—Catholic, Jewish, Methodist, Episcopal, Presbyterian, and Baptist—had published a joint statement calling for an end to the nonviolent demonstrations King was leading in Birmingham. They wrote, "We recognize the natural impatience of people who feel that their hopes are slow in being realized. But we are convinced that these demonstrations are unwise and untimely."[24] King's response was published in his 1964 book *Why We Can't Wait*. He wrote about his disappointment in the response of white churches and his refusal to "be patient" on their terms.

Their kind of patience was not a freely chosen witness to God's providence, but a weapon wielded by the powerful to shut down social change. Their kind of patience did not involve actively living the ways of God while expectantly awaiting God's coming reign. It involved slowing down the move toward justice because some people were afraid of losing their power and privilege. It emerged from fear and fed on fear. "Be patient, or else!" was the message. But King refused to give in to that kind of false patience. He wrote, "For years now I have heard the word 'Wait!' It rings in the ear of every Negro with piercing familiarity. This 'Wait' has almost always meant 'Never.' We must come to see, with one of our distinguished jurists, that 'justice too long delayed is justice denied'. . . . There comes a time when the cup of endurance runs over, and men are no longer willing to be plunged into the abyss of despair. I hope, sirs, you can understand our legitimate and unavoidable impatience."[25]

Despite King's clear and persuasive challenge to white versions of "patience," he embodied and encouraged another kind of patience. Rooted in his commitment to nonviolence, King refused to engage in an impatient call to arms. In his "I Have a Dream" speech, delivered on the steps of the Lincoln Memorial during the summer of 1963, King spoke of "the fierce urgency of now" and decried "the tranquilizing drug of gradualism." Yet he followed these words with a caveat:

> But there is something that I must say to my people who stand on the warm threshold which leads into the palace of justice. In the process of gaining our rightful place we must not be guilty of wrongful deeds. Let us not seek to satisfy our thirst for freedom by drinking from the cup of bitterness and hatred. We must forever conduct our struggle on the high plane of dignity and discipline. We must not allow our creative protest to degenerate into physical violence. [26]

King refused the kind of thoughtless impatience that gave in to the tyranny of emergency. His commitment to nonviolence meant that he was willing to take the time necessary to persuade the white population to change, rather than taking up arms in an attempt to force change. He recognized that white freedom and black freedom were "inextricably bound" and that "we cannot walk alone."[27] Thus, real transformation would require the kind of patience intrinsic to nonviolent action, the patience that seeks to change the heart of the oppressor and not just the law.

King's active patience was rooted in his belief in providence, his trust that "there is a creative force in this universe, working to pull down the gigantic mountains of evil, a power that is able to make a way out of no way and transform dark yesterdays into bright tomorrows." And so, he added, "Let us realize the arc of the moral universe is long but it bends toward justice."[28] The length of the arc means patience will be required, but the bending toward justice assures us that our patient action will not be in vain. Such conviction gave King the courage and the hope necessary to work for reconciliation and not just victory.

In a fearful culture, we will be tempted to act precipitously, which often means acting to control, coerce, or dominate. We will be tempted to think that every problem has to be resolved now or, preferably, yesterday. But that fearful push toward the rushed solution robs us of the patience we need to seek the right solution. As we learn to loosen the grip fear has on us, we will find ourselves able to embrace the patience necessary to be peacemakers. We will not be taken in by the rhetoric of "emergency time" that demands the quick (and often violent) fix. Nor will we be taken in by the rhetoric of false patience that urges inaction out of a fearful resistance to change. Only as we begin, once again, to trust the future will we be able to renounce unjust violence and false patience in order to embrace the vulnerable and patient discipline of peacemaking.

Questions for Discussion

1. In what ways does fear make it more difficult to live peacefully? Why do you think preemption is such a strong temptation?

2. Do you think most Americans believe that God is providentially guiding our country? Why do you think this belief is so strong among Americans? Is there a way of holding that belief without using it as a political tool? For instance, would it make a difference if we thought of God's providential guidance as a responsibility (aligning ourselves with God's plan for the good of the world) rather than a privilege (aligning God with our plans for the good of the nation)?

3. This chapter uses T. S. Eliot's play *Murder in the Cathedral* to help us think about the connection between providence and peace. Eliot says that we have to bear our "share of the eternal burden," which is also "the perpetual glory." But, he says, this burden/glory is just

"one moment," and another moment "shall pierce you with a sudden painful joy / When the figure of God's purpose is made complete." How do you interpret these lines? What is the burden we have to bear? What is the "figure of God's purpose"? How is all this connected to providence and peace? Why do you think Eliot links opposing ideas the way he does: "burden" and "glory," "painful" and "joy"?

4. Take a look at some of the scriptures mentioned in this chapter: James 4:1–3 and Matthew 26:47–52 (see the parallel account in Luke 22:47–51). Discuss these verses in their context. What do you see in these passages that speaks to the issues of fear, violence, and peacemaking?

5. Why do you think patience is so important for peacefulness? What makes it difficult for you to be patient? Are there cultural forces that work against patience? What could the church do to help its members develop patience?

6. How can we tell the difference between the true virtue of patience, that helps us be peaceful, and false patience, which is a kind of apathy that refuses to work for change?

10

The Risk of Generosity

■ One afternoon, after sharing a meal with some Pharisees, Jesus strolled outside to find a crowd of thousands gathered to see him and to hear his teachings. Someone in the crowd shouted out a request, "Teacher, tell my brother to divide the family inheritance with me" (Luke 12:13). But Jesus refused to become the arbiter between the brothers. Instead, he told the man, "Take care! Be on your guard against all kinds of greed; for one's life does not consist in the abundance of possessions" (12:15). He then told the crowd a parable about a rich man whose land had produced well beyond his expectations. The man was thrilled but faced a problem. He did not have enough space to store all the excess crops. So, he decided to raze his current barns and build new, bigger ones in their place. Once all of his goods were safely stored away, he would take his rest and say to himself, "Soul, you have ample goods laid up for many years; relax, eat, drink, be merry!" (12:19). But that very night he died.

The parable does not suggest that God killed the man for being greedy, but rather that his hoarding of goods, which was meant to secure his future for many years, ended up securing nothing. Jesus's teaching that "life does not consist in the abundance of possessions" says not only that possessions are not what makes life worth living, but that possessions cannot preserve or extend life. In my (admittedly rough) paraphrase, the point of the parable seems to be, "you may be rich, but you're still dead."

Jesus's attitude toward the rich fool, however, is not one of disdain but of compassion. We make a mistake if we read this parable as a parable of judgment, as if it implied that God was going to go around killing rich people for building big barns. This is a parable about someone who wrongly believed that great possessions could secure his future. It is a parable about fear and security and where true security lies. This message becomes clear if we read on in Luke's Gospel, for immediately following this parable Jesus says, "Therefore, do not worry about your life, what you will eat, or about your body, what you will wear. For life is more than food, and the body more than clothing. . . . And can any of you by worrying add a single hour to your span of life? If then you are not able to do so small a thing as that, why do you worry about the rest? . . . Do not be afraid, little flock, for it is your Father's good pleasure to give you the kingdom" (12:22–32). Jesus seeks to dispel the illusion that wealth can be a buffer against misfortune. When we trust in God's provision, we are able to release our fear of not getting by and so release our grip on possessions. "Strive for [God's] kingdom," Jesus tells the crowd, meaning, among other things, "sell your possessions and give alms." And if you do this, then "these things"—food, clothing, security—"will be given to you as well" (12:31–33). The highest good is God's kingdom, not our security, but if we seek God's kingdom, then God will provide for our security.

Beyond Accumulation

In a culture of fear, it is hard to believe that God is enough. We assume that if we don't make ourselves secure, no one will. And so we have become habituated to an ethic of safety. That is, we have begun to think of safety as the goal we should pursue above all others. I was recently reading about a report by the Council of Europe, the human rights arm of the EU, on the U.S. practice of "extraordinary rendition," sending prisoners to other countries for interrogation practices that would be illegal under U.S. law.[1] Whether, or to what extent, the United States does this is under dispute, but what was most interesting about the article was not its actual content. Rather, what caught my attention was a comment posted by a visitor to the BBC website in response to this story: "Whatever it takes to keep our world safe."[2] This belief that safety should be sought at all costs ("whatever it takes") has dire consequences. As we have seen, the ethic of safety fosters false virtues such as preemption and suspicion, which may seem to be virtuous if one's only goal is security; but if one's goal is to love God and neighbor, then such habits are destructive.

There is one more false virtue that we must unmask—the unbridled accumulation of wealth as a means of security. In fearful times we understandably wish to gather up whatever resources we can find to stave off the dangers that threaten. Biblical scholar Walter Brueggemann's analysis of our situation is insightful: "Today, the fundamental human condition continues to be anxiety, fueled by a market ideology that keeps pounding on us to take more, to not think about our neighbor, to be fearful, shortsighted, grudging. Over and over, we're told to be sure we have the resources to continue our affluent lifestyles, especially with the approach of our 'golden years' (which are 'golden' in more ways than one). . . . Whether it's global policies or local poverty-wage jobs, those who fear scarcity refuse to acknowledge any abundance that extends beyond their own coffers."[3]

Like the rich man in the parable, we imagine that accumulating wealth will make us more secure, and there is some truth to that. When we have inadequate resources, we rightly fear that the future may bring misfortunes that we cannot handle, such as high medical bills or an unexpected job layoff. However, this must be kept in perspective. In most cases, the practice of saving—for an emergency, or college, or retirement, for instance—reflects proper prudence and good stewardship of resources. The capacity to save reflects an ability to delay gratification and to resist the lure to buy more and more things. So the problem is not savings as such. The problem arises when our fear becomes excessive so that we can no longer make good judgments about what is enough, or when it causes us, in Aquinas's terms, to "renounce that which is good according to virtue."[4] When we are so intent to avoid harm to ourselves that we neglect to do good to others, then we have lost the battle with fear. So we sin not simply by accumulating savings, but by letting fear determine how much we need, by letting fear tighten our grip on wealth so that we neglect the call of Jesus to be generous.

How Providence Threatens Generosity

The culture of fear promotes the idea that the accumulation of wealth is a reasonable response to uncertain times. But if Christians are going to learn to hold our wealth loosely and to share our goods generously, we are going to have to be able to overcome inordinate fear. Above, I argued that trust in divine providence is one of the ways Christians can keep from being overwhelmed by fear. However, just as providence has been misused as a theological defense of violence and imperialism, so providence has been misused to justify the unbridled pursuit of financial self-interest. Unless we can combat this misuse of the doctrine, we will never develop the freedom to give generously as a Christian response to God's provision.

One of the most significant theorists of emerging capitalism was Adam Smith, an eighteenth-century Scottish moral philosopher. Smith believed that there were laws of economic life, just as there were laws of nature. And these economic laws worked in such a way that one best helped others by pursuing one's own financial self-interest. By seeking one's own security and wealth, one made others wealthier and more secure. Or to put it theologically, God so orders the means of economic provision that the pursuit of one's own good has the serendipitous effect of doing good to others. In a brief but momentous passage in his work *The Wealth of Nations,* Smith describes this idea in relation to the modern businessman:

> By preferring the support of domestic to that of foreign industry, he intends only his own security; and by directing that industry in such a manner as its produce may be of the greatest value, he intends only his own gain, and he is in this, as in many other cases, led by an invisible hand to promote an end which was no part of his intention. Nor is it always the worse for the society that it was not part of it. By pursuing his own interest he frequently promotes that of the society more effectually than when he really intends to promote it.[5]

Smith created the perfect economic philosophy for the modern age—all the calories, none of the guilt. This too-good-to-be-true philosophy was based on Smith's assumption that when we do something to promote our own gain or our own security, we often benefit others as a byproduct. So, for instance, the desire for wealth and greatness drives people "to cultivate the ground, to build houses, to found cities and commonwealths, and to invent and improve all the sciences and arts, which ennoble and embellish human life."[6] The goods of society and culture, including things like medicines, roads, and police forces, come into being because of the efforts of self-interested individuals, though at the same time they serve the good of others.

Smith went on to theorize that since a person can only consume so much of the earth's produce—noting that one person's stomach cannot hold substantially more than another person's—then even the rich landowner who harvests thousands of acres for his own gain can partake only of a small portion of that production. "The rest he is obliged to distribute among those, who prepare, in the nicest manner, that little which he himself makes use of, among those who fit up the palace in which this little is to be consumed, . . . all of whom thus derive from his luxury and caprice, that share of the necessaries of life, which they would in vain have expected from his humanity or his justice."[7] In other words, the livelihoods of all those who serve the rich man are dependent upon his continuing to seek greater and greater wealth, which, because he cannot consume all he produces, will inevitably redound to their benefit. This,

Smith concludes, indicates that there is an invisible hand, "providence," that keeps the economic balance even as we all live self-interested lives. He writes that the wealthy "are led by an invisible hand to make nearly the same distribution of the necessaries of life, which would have been made, had the earth been divided into equal portions among all its inhabitants, and thus without intending it, without knowing it, advance the interest of the society." Again, Smith exhibits a remarkable trust in the combined effects of the market and the natural limits of human consumption to create an equal distribution of goods among people. He goes on to attribute this directly to providence: "When Providence divided the earth among a few lordly masters, it neither forgot nor abandoned those who seemed to have been left out in the partition. These last too enjoy their share of all that it produces."[8]

Contrary to classical or Christian moral theory, Smith suggests that one can serve the common good without having to develop the virtues of charity, temperance, self-control, or justice. Indeed, he suggests we might even serve the interests of society best, or at least "more effectually," when we are not explicitly trying to do so. Smith's theories have produced in modern times what theologian John Milbank has called the "de-ethicization" of the economic.[9] Rather than reflecting on the moral issues involved in making and spending, producing and consuming, Smith's theories appealed to "providence" to explain "how bad or self-interested actions can have good long-term outcomes."[10] Thus, we need not entertain the ethical questions, since matters of equity and justice should naturally work themselves out.

Providence came to serve as an excuse *not* to engage in practices of generosity, not to follow the self-giving path of the cross, not to put the needs of others before one's own. Rather than strengthening a courageous and patient life of Christian discipleship, Smith's providence made traditional morality seem archaic and unnecessary. Interpreted through this lens, providence assures us that God will take care of the poor if we just take care of ourselves. One of the ironies here is that by bringing God *into* the discussion of economy, by appealing to the doctrine of providence, it became more difficult to use providence to critique the market. The language had already been captured.

This de-ethicization of the economic was even reflected in some Christian preaching of the early modern period. Sociologist Max Weber, writing in the early twentieth century, detected in some seventeenth-century English sermons "the comforting assurance that the unequal distribution of the goods of this world was a special dispensation of Divine Providence, which in these differences, as in particular grace, pursued secret ends unknown to men."[11] Again the assumption is that inequality arises from God's decision rather than from human injustice or exploitation. Understood in this way, providence releases us from all moral obligations with regard to wealth and the marketplace, since ultimately God must have reasons for keeping the poor poor. Providence becomes an excuse for inaction.

We might note, briefly, that capitalism, understood as an unrestrained free market, does not seem to function the way Smith thought it would. Perhaps the invisible hand has gotten tired of working its magic. As far back as the time of Jesus, people were aware that the wealthy did not necessarily share their goods with others (or even sell them to others) just because they could not consume all that they had produced. Rather, the human inclination is to build bigger barns, to find ways to store and amass goods for the future, to amass even more than one could conceivably need, since one might need little but want much. Especially when fear of the future combines with self-interested production, we cannot expect that the self-interested pursuit of gain will result in an equitable distribution of goods, even for basic needs.

Provision, Abundance, and Generosity

In scripture and tradition, before the rise of modernity and capitalism, the doctrine of providence did not constitute a social safety net that freed us from moral obligations to one another. Rather, as I have argued above, providence was meant to assure us of God's continuing care for us so that we might share generously with others. Following Jesus means embracing an ethic of risk; it tells us to imitate God's radical generosity, trusting that the rest will be provided to us.

The Book of Genesis offers an interesting example of the tension between trusting God's providential care and exploiting others for personal gain.[12] Genesis begins with abundance and ends with scarcity. It begins with creation, God's abundant giving of being. It ends with a famine that drives the Israelites down to Egypt to avoid starvation. The movement from abundance to scarcity creates the opportunity for God's people to decide how they are going to handle the threat of "not enough." The text recognizes that the real issue is not the natural scarcity produced by famine, but what human beings are willing and ready to do in the face of that scarcity. In the narrative, Joseph, one of Jacob's twelve sons, has been sold by his brothers into slavery. The slave traders take Joseph to Egypt, where he is arrested and jailed on false charges. Ultimately, Joseph gains his freedom because God has gifted him with the ability to interpret dreams. As it turns out, the Pharaoh needs just such a person. Joseph's interpretation of Pharaoh's dreams suggests that there will be a period of abundance followed by a period of famine. In response, Pharaoh asks

Joseph to create a plan to keep the people fed during the lean years. So far, so good. God has made it possible for Joseph and Pharaoh to prepare for the coming scarcity in such a way that God's abundant provision will be enough—even when the land is barren.

At this point the story takes a dark turn. Rather than meeting scarcity with abundance, Joseph and Pharaoh choose to exploit scarcity to gain even more for themselves. Their scheme works like this. For seven years Joseph collects one-fifth of the produce of the land and stores it away in advance of the coming lean years. When the famine hits, Joseph sells a portion of the extra grain back to the people of Egypt and Canaan for exorbitant prices. Indeed, the text says that he "collected all the money to be found in the land of Egypt and in the land of Canaan, in exchange for the grain" (Gen. 47:14). The next year, Joseph requires payment of "all their livestock" in exchange for the grain (47:17). The following year, as the famine continues, Joseph requires the people to give up all their land and finally to sell themselves into slavery to Pharaoh. "All the Egyptians sold their fields, because the famine was severe upon them; and the land became Pharaoh's. As for the people, he made slaves of them from one end of Egypt to the other" (47:20–21).

What began as a plan to gather and share the abundance of God in order to prevent scarcity ended as a plan to exploit scarcity so that Pharaoh could accumulate all the wealth and land in the kingdom. Joseph, as Pharaoh's partner, had effectively collected the excess from the people for seven years only to sell their own extra produce back to them at such an exorbitant rate that they were forced to become slaves in order to eat. The truth is, there was no real scarcity. God's provision created enough abundance to carry the people through the drought. The scarcity came from Pharaoh's determination not to open the storehouses freely to the people but to sell them back what was rightfully theirs to begin with.

Brueggemann interprets Pharaoh's actions this way: "Because Pharaoh . . . is afraid that there aren't enough good things to go around, he must try to have them all. Because he is fearful, he is ruthless."[13] The contrast between God's abundance and our fear of scarcity continues to be a defining issue for us today. If, like Pharaoh and Joseph, we are incapable of trusting God's abundance, then we will take advantage of the threat of scarcity to line our own pockets, to secure our own futures at the expense of others. In contrast, if we believe that God can and will provide abundantly, then we will be able to "live according to an ethic whereby we are not driven, controlled, anxious, frantic or greedy, precisely because we are sufficiently at home and at peace to care about others as we have been cared for."[14] Trusting providence means trusting God's provision, and trusting in God's provision allows us to embody generosity.

139

After the scheme by Pharaoh and Joseph, after the Israelites find themselves enslaved in Egypt, after Moses brings them to freedom across the Red Sea, the Bible tells a very different story of scarcity and abundance. As the Israelites are wandering through the desert, making their way to the Promised Land, they grow tired and hungry. Some of them even want to turn back to Egypt, back to the devil they know. The hot, dry desert is a place of scarcity, and even though Egypt was a place of oppression, at least they had food. So God tells Moses, "I am going to rain bread from heaven for you and each day the people shall go out and gather enough for that day" (Exod. 16:4). God answers scarcity with abundance but makes very clear that the abundance depends on the Israelites' practicing restraint. Each person is to gather only as much bread, or "manna," as he or she needs and to leave the rest for others. In this way, God promises there will be enough. Many of the Israelites did what God commanded, "some gathering more, some less. But when they measured it . . . those who gathered much had nothing over, and those who gathered little had no shortage; they gathered as much as each of them needed" (Exod. 16:17–18). Yet having been shaped in Egypt by the logic of scarcity, some of the Israelites tried to gather more than they needed, to save and accumulate for later. Not only did this leave others hungry, but it proved wasteful, since the extra bread spoiled overnight and became useless. In God's economy, hoarding would not be rewarded.

This story functions as parable of living into the gift of divine provision. It teaches us to trust that God's economy is indeed abundant, even in the midst of apparent scarcity, but we subvert that abundance when we seek to gather more than we need while others have less than they need. "Trust in God's providence therefore involves not only an expectation of sustenance," writes Christopher Franks, "but also a yielding of ourselves, whereby we conform our demands for sustenance to the temporally unfolding determination of that provision."[15] In other words, providence is not only about God providing for our needs but also about our learning to need no more than God provides.

When we get to the New Testament we find the apostle Paul using similar logic to encourage the Corinthians to contribute generously to the offering for the poor in Jerusalem. Paul assures them, "God is able to provide you with every blessing in abundance, so that by always having enough of everything, you may share abundantly in every good work" (2 Cor. 9:8). God gives abundantly not just so that they will have enough, but so that they will be able to participate in the joy of sharing God's abundance with others. As in the story of manna in the desert, the reality of abundance for all requires not only God's provision but human participation in the just distribution of the abundance God has provided.

John Calvin has often been credited with paving the way for the economic shifts of modernity—opening theological space for a free market and lending at interest. Whether or not this is a fair assessment, what has been less noted in his writing is the way that he connects God's generosity toward us with a kind of radical economic sharing. This path of generosity begins, he affirms, with the acknowledgment that "all the gifts we possess have been bestowed by God and entrusted to us on condition that they be distributed for our neighbors' benefit."[16] Our goods come to us conditionally; thus, nothing we have may be considered our own in any ultimate sense. Scripture and tradition support the idea of *personal* property but not *private* property; that is, property may be personal in the sense of being under my control, but it is not private in the sense that what I do with it is purely my own concern. If, as the psalmist tells us, "the earth is the Lord's and all that is in it" (Ps. 24:1), then all human ownership is really a kind of stewardship—that is, a trust to manage the goods of another.

Thus, Calvin notes, "Scripture calls us to resign ourselves and all our possessions to the Lord's will."[17] Of course, part of "the Lord's will" involves meeting our needs and those of our families. So, the question arises, how much do we need? How much is enough? According to Calvin, we must first "yield to [God] the desires of our hearts to be tamed,"[18] if we are going to be able to distribute our gifts for our neighbors' benefit. For until we learn to temper our desires, that is, to know the difference between wants and needs, we will always find justification for gratifying our wants while others go without needs. As long as our desires have no limits, we will never know how to say "enough." Yet living in a consumer-driven society, we are daily bombarded with advertising intended to stimulate our desires and magnify our fears so that we lose the ability to distinguish want and need.

Control or Flow?

So if I've convinced you that we need to reclaim the practice of generosity in this culture of fear, what should that generosity look like? Is generosity the same as giving charity, or as they used to say, "almsgiving"? Certainly generosity needs to include a voluntary redistribution of resources from those who have more than they need to those who have less than they need. But charity can have unintended consequences. First, we may use charitable giving as an excuse not to change social arrangements that make it difficult for the poor to break out of poverty and attain the dignity of self-supporting work (as when Wal-Mart makes large donations to local charities rather than paying a living wage). Second, charitable giving may produce a habit of dependence among those who receive assistance as well as an opportunity for control among those who give it.

The biblical story of two brothers, Cain and Abel, provides some interesting reflections on care and responsibility. After murdering Abel, Cain famously asked God, "Am I my brother's keeper?" (Gen. 4:9).[19] Some of us still assume that the answer is yes, although increasingly this is a minority view in the culture. We sometimes hear people quote this passage as a way of calling us to a proper concern for the welfare of our fellow human beings. But the biblical text suggests something different is going on. The word "keeper" is never used in Genesis (nor anywhere in Torah) to describe something humans should do or be for each other. Human beings "keep" flocks or "keep" the covenant, but they do not "keep" each other. By contrast, God alone is described as "keeping" people, for instance, when God tells Jacob, "Know that I am with you and will keep you wherever you go" (Gen. 28:15). So, Cain seems to be reminding God that God is his brother's keeper and that God, not Cain, should be watching out for Abel. If something has happened to Abel, Cain implies, it's God's fault. Cain thus speaks a half-truth. By throwing back on God the responsibility of "keeping" Abel, Cain rightly recognizes that we cannot be God to each other, but falsely assumes that this fact releases us from all responsibility.

When we think of practicing generosity or charity, we have to be careful neither to imagine ourselves as our brother's keeper (thus asserting a control over the other that is not rightly ours), nor to suggest that since God is our brother's keeper, we have no moral obligations. As we have already seen, the abundance of provision comes from God alone, but God relies on us to participate in God's abundance in such a way that we do not hoard the blessing. We have a part in keeping the blessing flowing, becoming a conduit for God's abundance. Which is to say we are called to be our brother's brother, our sister's sister, so that God can be their keeper.

In the closing voiceover of the film *American Beauty*, Lester Burnham, the main character, who has just died in the story, speaks of the revelation that accompanied his death. These words suggest to me something about generosity; they give me a way of viewing generosity as participating in the "flow" of beauty. Generosity happens when we release control and become a conduit of blessing (which is, I think, the fullness of beauty). Lester explains, "I guess I could be pretty pissed off about what happened to me, but it's hard to stay mad when there's so much beauty in the world. Sometimes I feel like I'm seeing it all at once, and it's too much, my heart fills up like a balloon that's about to burst. And then I remember to relax, and stop trying to hold on to it, and then it flows through me like rain and I can't feel anything but gratitude for every single moment of my stupid little life."[20] Generosity has to do with our capacity to get caught up in this flow of something bigger than ourselves, to imagine ourselves as a portal of divine abundance. Rightly understood, divine providence frees us of our illusions of control for the sake of God's abundant charity. In so doing we may also invite others to participate in the unhindered flow of God's goods.

Generous Business

The vision of generosity I am sketching here is not simply personal or private. What we need in today's economy are examples of people carrying this trust in abundance, this flow of generosity, into their business practices. By that I do not mean simply that businesses should make large donations to worthy causes (though that's not a bad thing); rather, I mean businesses should build the habits and practices of generosity into the process of producing and selling goods. We need to be able to see, describe, and imagine doing business in such a way that we refuse to make profit our highest goal, thus focusing our work on the shared good that is produced both for the workers and the buyers. Generous business, or what some are calling "humane capitalism,"[21] refuses to create wealth for some at the expense of others but trusts that God has given enough abundance for everyone to have what they need. The job of generous business is to participate in the flow of that abundance.

One inspiring example of generous business is craigslist.org, an online community of classified ads and discussion forums that serves as "a place to find jobs, housing, goods & services, social activities, a girlfriend or boyfriend, advice, community information, and just about anything else—all for free, and in a relatively non-commercial environment."[22] The list began as Craig Newmark's online list of activities going on in the San Francisco area. Over time the site grew, and when Newmark wrote software that could turn e-mails into Web posts, he opened the site to postings from others. The site quickly became a nexus for thousands of job listings, apartment rentals, items for sale, personals—typical classified material. In addition, the site created a sense of community through discussion forums and occasional face-to-face parties. What made this site different from other such services was that Newmark didn't charge anything, nor did he allow ads on the site. The endeavor made no money. In 1997 he was approached by Microsoft Sidewalk with an offer to run banner ads. Though he could have quit his day job and lived off of the revenue of that one customer, Newmark declined the offer.[23]

In 1999 he decided to devote all his energy to craigslist and turned it into a for-profit company. Holding onto the goal of providing a non-commercial environment, Newmark still did not allow advertising on the site. Instead, he began to charge minimal rates (well below market value) for job listings in San Francisco, Los Angeles, and New York. Because of the incredible volume of the site, this income alone has supported the company. Though he could make a lot more profit from the service than he does, Newmark says, quite simply, "We're not looking to make a lot of money."[24] The significance of this statement only becomes clear when you begin to add up what the site *could* make.

Craigslist is used by more than 10 million people per month, covers over 190 cities, posts more than 9 million classified ads per month and over 400,000 new job listings each month.[25] Experts believe the site could be sold for up to $100 million.[26] Short of that, the site could begin charging for job listings in other major cities, such as Atlanta, Boston, Chicago, or Miami, where the service is still free. The title of a 2004 *New York Times* article says it all: "Craig's To-Do List: Leave Millions on the Table."[27] The article goes on to describe Newmark as "a man committed to a goal most entrepreneurs would revile: he has steadfastly avoided maximizing his commercial success."[28] Newmark recognizes that any attempt to maximize profit would come at the expense of his vision for the kind of service he wants to provide. That service gets defined on the craigslist website in this way:

- giving each other a break, getting the word out about everyday, real-world stuff
- restoring the human voice to the Internet, in a humane, non-commercial environment
- keeping things simple, common-sense, down-to-earth, honest, very real
- providing an alternative to impersonal, big-media sites
- being inclusive, giving a voice to the disenfranchised, democratizing
- being a collection of communities with similar spirit, not a single monolithic entity[29]

Discussion of profit does not make its way onto this list. It is rightly understood as a byproduct of doing work that is worth doing.

Craigslist displays the flow of generosity that we've discussed in this chapter. When asked about why he has not "cashed in" on the site (a question often asked by incredulous interviewers), Newmark has several responses. He believes, for instance, that "some things should be about money, some shouldn't." [30] Such an answer is refreshing coming from a for-profit business owner in a market culture where everything, we assume, ought to have a price. On his blog, he credits the music and poetry of Leonard Cohen for his refusal to cash in.[31] And yet another answer is that he just doesn't need that much. Here is a guy who seems to know what it is to have enough. "Until recently," he says, "the only thing lacking in my life was a regular parking place (I live in a city), but since my move, all I want is a hummingbird feeder that hummingbirds actually like."[32] Rather than fearful accumulation, craigslist reflects a willingness to acknowledge that some things are more important than money, that ultimately there will be enough, and that doing business involves not just making money but participating in a communal endeavor for the good of all involved. And it does this while being successful and sustainable by anyone's standards.

Sabbath Living

What resources does the church have to offer to help us regain generosity in a culture of fear? Traditionally, the practice of Sabbath-keeping was one way the church (and the synagogue) developed the virtues necessary to engage in courageous generosity. The challenge is to reclaim Sabbath, not just as a set of practices surrounding a single day of the week, but as a way of living, a daily trust in God's abundance, that nurtures patience, peace, and gratitude. Brueggemann points us in the right direction when he writes, "As shown in the creation account, Sabbath (God's day of rest) is based on abundance. But how willing are we to practice Sabbath? A Sabbath spent catching up on chores we were too busy to do during the week is hardly a testimony to abundance. A Sabbath spent encouraging those who want to fill our 'free time' with calls to amass more possessions—whether the malls with their weekend specials or televised sports events with their clutter of commercials—does nothing to weaken the domain of scarcity. Honoring the Sabbath is a form of witness. It tells the world that 'there is enough.'"[33]

Sabbath-keeping is a way of practicing providence, of enacting the belief that God will provide. One day each week, we give up providing for ourselves, we do not work or strive or struggle to get more things or secure our future. On this day, we practice the kind of reliance on God that can sustain our generosity throughout the rest of the week. But Sabbath is more than a day, or better put, it is a day that gestures beyond itself to other habits and practices that support God's economy in everyday living.

For the ancient Israelites, one of these practices was the sabbatical year (Exod. 23:10–13; Lev. 25:1–7; Deut. 15:1–18). Every seventh year the Israelites were commanded to give rest to the land, to let their fields lie fallow. In this year the poor and the wild animals were given free access

145

to whatever the land produced. Further, within the community of God's people, all debts were wiped clean and all slaves were set free. In addition to the Sabbath day and the sabbatical year, there was one more grand gesture of God's abundance built into Israel's Torah—the Jubilee Year. This was a Sabbath of Sabbath years—seven times seven years. In this forty-ninth year not only did all the sabbatical-year regulations apply, but all land was returned to its original owner. If a family had fallen on hard times and had to sell their land to buy food or pay debt, the Jubilee Year assured that this would not create for that family a cycle of poverty extending through many generations. Rather, every Jubilee provided a chance to start over, every Jubilee broke the back of poverty and returned to all the people the means of production. The central features of the Sabbath economy, rest and plenty, were evident throughout Israel's economic life.

The goal of these practices was a periodic restructuring of the economy so that the gap between rich and poor would not continue to grow unchecked. In the context of explaining the sabbatical regulations, Moses tells the people, "There will, however, be no one in need among you, because the Lord is sure to bless you in the land that the Lord your God is giving you as a possession to occupy, if only you will obey the Lord your God by diligently observing this entire commandment that I command you today" (Deut. 15:4–5). Note the "if only"—God's promise of provision is based on Israel's willingness to live in a Sabbath-based economy, that is, an economy of abundance and trust. The text goes on to say that when an Israelite releases a slave in the sabbatical year, he or she is to be provided for: "You shall not send him out empty-handed. Provide liberally out of your flock, your threshing-floor, and your wine press, thus giving to him some of the bounty with which the Lord your God has blessed you" (Deut. 15:13–14). The abundance of God is to be held lightly, permitted to flow through the hands of those who have much, to bring blessing to those who have little.

The Christian celebration of the Eucharist recalls and enacts the logic of divine abundance that permeates the sabbatical regulations. Echoing the feeding of the multitudes, Jesus at the Last Supper took bread, gave thanks, blessed the bread, and broke it. And as he broke the bread and gave it to others, there was enough—enough for the five thousand hungry followers, enough for the twelve disciples, enough for us. The bread and wine of Communion is a continuation of Jesus's miraculous provision whereby he, himself, becomes our food. It is a foretaste of God's heavenly feast and a promise that God's provision will never be lacking. But, as we have seen, this divine provision is enough for all only if we do not subvert God's abundance by hoarding the blessing. Christians are sent from the Eucharist to share with the world what we have received at the table—bread broken and enough for all. We are sent to tell the world, "Do not be afraid . . . for it is your Father's good pleasure to give you the kingdom" (Luke 12:32).

Questions for Discussion

1. What do you think of the comment from the BBC website, "Whatever it takes to keep our world safe"? Do you agree? If not, then where do you place limits, what can we *not* do to keep our world safe?
2. Read through some of the biblical passages from the chapter (Gen. 47:13–26; Exod. 16:1–30; Lev. 25:1–7; Deut. 15:1–18; Luke 12:13–34). How does scripture invite us to think about wealth, work, economy, and generosity, especially in relation to our fears about having (or not having) enough?
3. How do you determine what is enough when it comes to the accumulation of wealth through savings and investments? Do you have anyone you can talk freely with about stewardship of money? Why do you think Americans are so reticent to talk about money (how much we make, spend, save, and give), even though we find it increasingly easy to talk about other personal matters, like sex?
4. Had you heard of Adam Smith's "invisible hand" before reading this chapter? Do you think there is any truth to his theory that we help others best when we pursue our self-interest? Can you think of examples where the pursuit of self-interest actually harms others?
5. In a culture of fear we are all the more tempted to be controlling—to control our money, to control other people, to control the future. How does providence help us release control? What church rituals or sacraments help us practice giving up control? How does giving up control help us become generous?
6. Can you think of examples of everyday generosity from your life or others you know? How do we (or how might we) let God's abundance "flow" through us in ordinary living?
7. This book begins and ends with the biblical words, "Do not be afraid." What will you take away with you after reading this book that will help you be less fearful? How can Christians live in the world in such a way that we help others around us to be less fearful?

Appendix: The Deep Roots of Fear

■ To understand fear in the present, we need to understand our past. Thus, this appendix takes a deeper look at some of the historical and philosophical roots of the culture of fear. Though the discussion is perhaps more philosophically abstract than other parts of the book, I have tried to make these complex ideas as accessible as possible. This analysis matters because it helps us understand why we are so susceptible to fear-based manipulation. I argue that many of our particular fears in the present arise out of underlying cultural (and ultimately spiritual) insecurities from our past. With that in mind, I will focus this appendix around three "deep roots" of fear:

1. Political roots: modern political theories that rely on fear as a foundation for politics.
2. Cultural roots: the diminishing confidence that the world has a coherent story (much less a happy ending).
3. Theological roots: our flight from God and our desire to be self-creators (a lesson learned from an ancient story in a garden).

The Pope, the Prince, and the Bourgeoisie

The roots of Western democracies stretch back to the period of the Enlightenment in the seventeenth century, when European nations were beginning to organize themselves as independent political bodies after the demise of the Holy Roman Empire. In contrast to the long preceding period of church rule, these emerging nations imagined a new kind of politics based not on a common faith or a common vision of what is good, but on procedures of justice and the priority of individual freedom.

This emphasis on freedom led political philosophers to call this new politics "liberalism" (from the Latin root *liber,* meaning "free"). Throughout this chapter, I will use the word *liberalism* in this broad sense—not as a description of the left wing of the Democratic Party, but as a description of those modern forms of democratic governance in the West, including the United States, that make individual freedom the highest good. *Liberalism* as a term of political theory describes our form of government, not a particular partisan viewpoint. (Thus, a right-wing Republican might prove to be the most "liberal" by seeking to maximize individual freedoms while limiting the role of the state.)

This new kind of politics resulted from two related factors in the sixteenth and seventeenth centuries. First were the religious wars. The battles between Catholics and Protestants convinced many in Europe that there would be no way to create peace without creating a political system where people were allowed to disagree on religious matters. Second was the rise of the nation-state. As the Holy Roman Empire fractured, different political players struggled to claim power—pope, emperor, royalty, nobility, and the bourgeoisie. The independent nations of Europe—France, Germany, England, etc.—emerged out of these wars. The interplay of religious strife and political maneuvering was quite complex, and it became unclear at times whether a particular war was being fought for religious or political purposes.[1] What evolved out of this complex period of social change was a kind of political system in which people agreed to disagree about the big questions of truth and goodness (because these were, at their core, religious questions), focusing instead on the procedural questions of justice, rights, and freedoms.

There were, of course, both gains and losses in this transformation, but what is interesting here is the way that fear was used to make sense of the new political order. Admittedly, fear was already being used as a political tool in the Middle Ages—fear of crossing the emperor, the prince, or the feudal lord kept people in line, while fear of hell kept people in church. However, with the rise of democracy, the fear of those above us in the social hierarchy was largely replaced by a more generalized fear of our neighbors. To put it simply, fear of tyranny was replaced by fear of anarchy.

Why did the people fear anarchy? Because they were trying to create political communities, nations, that did not rely on a shared religious faith. And if they could not assume a shared belief in religious matters like "Who are we?" "Where are we going?" and "What is the good we should seek?" then they were going to have to deal with the problem of unity: "What makes us 'us'?" and "What can bring us together and unite us in a common cause, if we cannot assume agreement on the most basic matters of life?" This is where fear played an important role. The philosophers and politicians of the day began to wonder, if people cannot be united by the goods they pursue, can they be united by the evils they avoid?

Thomas Hobbes and the Politics of Fear

The idea that fear is the glue that holds us together was explored best by the English philosopher Thomas Hobbes. The son of a parish priest, Hobbes was born in 1588, just as the Spanish were trying to invade England. Indeed, as he tells the story, his mother went into premature labor upon hearing of the approaching Spanish Armada. "Fear and I were born twins," he observed.[2] Having held off the Spanish during Hobbes's childhood, the English devolved into civil war during his adulthood. In his writings Hobbes seemed intent to stave off both the fear into which he was born and the chaos through which he lived. He did this by working out a political philosophy that sought to shore up the foundation of social order.

Hobbes began by trying to imagine how people came to enter into community. What caused us to be social creatures rather than loners? Surely human social order reflects something more than the instinct that leads wolves to hunt in packs. But what is that something? Hobbes surmised that the roots of political life evolved from a primal state in which isolated individuals each pursued their own survival and self-interest at the expense of everyone else. It was, in the beginning, a war of "every man against every man."[3] Without some kind of social agreement, this situation could only produce a life of fear that was "solitary, poor, nasty, brutish, and short."[4]

In the primal story as Hobbes imagined it, human beings, out of fear and self-interest, finally decided to relinquish the right to use violence against each other. They placed the enforcement of this agreement in the hands of a governing person or body, who would be the only one allowed to use force. Thus, he imagines, politics exists not to organize people to pursue some goods in common, but to protect us from each other. The real threat is not (first of all) outside enemies, but the violent anarchy that lurks just beneath the surface of social order. The basis of any true society, says Hobbes, is our "mutual fear" of each other.[5] Hobbes's ideas were not the only attempt to provide a rationale for the politics of the new nations, but they remain one of the most important attempts, in that they take seriously the problem of creating political unity where there is religious disagreement.

The systems of democratic governance that have emerged in the modern West since Hobbes's time, including that in the United States, are not exactly what Hobbes imagined, but they have largely continued to rely on fear as a rationale for political unity. As a least common denominator, the fear of loss and death provided, and still provides, that common link that can bring a people together—not around a shared good that we pursue in common but around a shared evil that we avoid in common. While there were practical reasons to propose this view of politics, a reliance on fear for unity may create more problems than it solves.

The Politics of Fear Today: Talking Back to Hobbes

Though Hobbes wrote in the seventeenth century, his ideas about fear and politics remain part of our political conversations. I want to look briefly at two contemporary views on the subject. The first, that of Judith Shklar, supports the idea that we can and should seek political unity on the basis of fear. The second, that of Corey Robin, critiques a fear-based politics as dangerous and self-defeating.

Judith Shklar (1928–1992) was a leading political theorist and a professor of government at Harvard University. She wrote a famous essay, "The Liberalism of Fear," in 1989, in which she argued that modern liberal politics "does not, to be sure, offer a *summum bonum* [greatest good] toward which all political agents should strive, but it certainly does begin with a *summum malum* [greatest evil], which all of us know and would avoid if only we could."[6] She identifies this "greatest evil" as "cruelty," which is "the willful inflicting of physical pain on a weaker being in order to cause anguish and fear."[7] She argues that a liberal political system must rely on our common fear of cruelty to provide social cohesion.

Shklar's own early life may have influenced her views on these matters. I imagine she could echo Hobbes's claim "Fear and I were born twins." Shklar was born in Riga, Latvia, in 1928, but by the late 1930s the city had become a hostile place. As she put it, "We were essentially German Jews, which meant that almost everyone around us wanted us to be somewhere else at best, or to kill us at worst."[8] Just before the Russians arrived in Latvia in 1939, her family fled to Sweden, and after the German invasion of Norway, they took the Trans-Siberian railway to Japan. They finally found refuge in Canada, after being locked up in Seattle "for several surrealistic weeks in a detention jail for illegal Oriental immigrants."[9] Her journey led her to Harvard for graduate study in political theory, and she stayed on as a professor there for the rest of her life.

Shklar writes that she "took up political theory as a way of making sense of the experiences of the 20th century. What had brought us to such a pass? In one way or another that question has lurked behind everything I have written."[10] Much of her early work focused on the question "How are we to think about the Nazi era?"[11] Her response was to think of it as precisely the kind of cruelty that a liberal political system should help us avoid. Modern liberalism holds us together because we all fear that kind of cruelty. She believes that if we ask our political system to do more than deliver us from this fear, we move all too quickly toward fascism and communism and other "-isms" that justify cruelty for the sake of ideology. Shklar advocates a "liberalism of fear" not because it is the highest political aspiration, but because she believes it is the most we can safely hope to agree on.

In contrast, Corey Robin, a young political philosopher at Brooklyn College, challenges the idea that fear can serve a useful, foundational function in a political system. Unlike Shklar, who was profoundly shaped by the events in Europe during World War II, Robin's political thought emerges out of a post-9/11 American context. He argues that embracing fear as a unifying political force ultimately undermines our ability to address the very things we are afraid of.

> Convinced that we lack moral or political principles to bind us together, we savor the experience of being afraid, as many writers did after 9/11, for only fear, we believe, can turn us from isolated men and women into a unified people. Looking to political fear as the ground of our public life, we refuse to see the grievances and controversies that underlie it. We blind ourselves to the real-world conflicts that make fear an instrument of political rule and advance, deny ourselves the tools that might mitigate those conflicts, and ultimately ensure that we stay in thrall to fear.[12]

The problem, Robin argues, is that when we rely on fear for political unity, we too easily come to manipulate fear for political power. Keeping a people in thrall to fear serves the interests of those who hold power, precisely because a fearful people will seek order and stability. In practice this can mean you are less likely to get voted out of office if people are afraid, because change will appear threatening. Of course, this is a delicate balancing act, because people need to believe both that the threats are perpetual and that their leaders are keeping the threats at bay. Thus, those who hold power have an incentive to perpetuate the sense of danger, since fear benefits those who claim to protect us.

Perhaps this is why it has been said that there is nothing wrong with America that a good war will not fix. We never feel as focused and unified as when we have a common enemy. This truth is not lost on our politicians, who are always ready to ratchet up the fear rhetoric and rally the voters against a common threat (whether that "threat" is gays and illegal immigrants, as some Republicans would argue, or the Iraq War and the curtailing of civil liberties, as some Democrats would argue). The fact that flag-burning amendments seem to pop up regularly around election time suggests that someone is gaining political capital from the "threat" posed by flag burners. Such political posturing works because it galvanizes a certain constituency around a shared enemy, even if this enemy does not represent the most pressing political concern.

Robin argues that a liberalism based on fear will undermine itself by reproducing the very fear it claims to defeat. He refers to American liberalism as "schizophrenic,"[13] a "double-edged sword,"[14] and a "contradictory inheritance,"[15] because even as it claims to tame our fears, it both relies on fear for social unity and exploits fear to quell social change. Unfortunately, Robin does not provide a convincing alternative foundation for social unity. He suggests that justice, freedom, or equality could serve as better defining ideals than fear, but he does not answer the fundamental questions concerning these ideals: whose account of justice? whose definition of freedom? whose vision of equality? The very reason fear became an important political foundation in the modern West was that the common worldview of the Middle Ages had broken down and could not be repaired.

What Robin does not seem to consider is the possibility that he and Shklar are both right. He is right that using fear as a political foundation is ultimately threatening to positive goods such as justice, freedom, and equality, but Shklar is also right that shared fear is the only pragmatic foundation for a political system that does not presume a common religious tradition or worldview among its citizens. Perhaps, then, there is a deep contradiction embedded in modern democratic societies, to which Robin has hinted with his references to the "schizophrenia" and the "double-edged sword" of American politics. Ultimately, I would argue, the way to overcome a fear-based politics is not going to be a better political theory but a better theology.

Losing the Big Story: No More Happy Endings

Our world today is far more fragmented than it was in Hobbes's time. In the United States, for instance, our population is so broad and diverse that we can presume very few shared convictions, stories, or practices. We seem fated to rely on fear to create unity, because it seems to be the only foundation we can find once we recognize that we have no shared story. Or, to put it another way, fear becomes the story we share in the absence of any other shared account of goods and goals.

If we lack a political story sufficient to bind us all together in a common cause, it is but an indication of a wider cultural shift.[16] Many self-described "postmodern" people have begun to despair of, or even to grow suspicious of, living in a "storied world." That is, fewer and fewer people believe that history constitutes a coherent narrative with a beginning, a middle, and an end, since this kind of coherence suggests there must be some kind of "author" of the story (either God, humankind, or nature). The idea that our lives are part of a larger drama strikes many as wishful (and not particularly plausible) thinking. Or worse, some suspect that all the grand stories of history are just tools of power—certain people telling stories that bolster their claims to dominance and privilege. Even if history *does* have a story, they might say, it seems as likely to have a bad ending as a good one.

Many today find it hard to trust the future since the present feels more and more like "just one d-mn thing after another." On the personal level, many despair of finding a unified thread in their lives and instead experience each day as a somewhat random chain of events that have no necessary connection to what went before or what comes after. The practice among young people of "hooking up" for one-night sexual encounters reflects just this sense that even the most intimate emotional moments stand disconnected from a past and a future. And without a sense of life as a story that is unfolding, building to some conclusion, it becomes difficult to know how (or why) to sustain commitments and promises.

Prior to the advent of modernity, most people believed the world had a story because the world had an author. History is God's story, they would have said, and while humans are capable of creating confusion during the middle scenes of the drama, God never ceases to guide and direct the creation to its good end. The plotline may seem vague at times, even threatened, but it never devolves into chaos or randomness. People could trust time and history because they trusted that the God who created the world would finally reconcile all things. The shifting sands of modernity and postmodernity have challenged this way of experiencing time and history. Instead of reading history as God's story, we have increasingly come to interpret history as a purely human story or as no story at all.

To help you understand this loss of story, I have to tell you a story about the rise of modernity. Modern people did not begin by doubting that history was progressing toward a good goal. In fact, the seventeenth and eighteenth centuries ushered in a long period of optimism and trust in human progress. Advances in science and medicine allowed us to tame certain natural threats. Advances in technology made work easier and leisure time more abundant. Up through the nineteenth century the narrative of human progress held our imaginations and gave us hope for the future. Karl Marx provided an economic narrative of social progress that moved inevitably toward the formation of a good and just society, and Charles Darwin gave us a biological narrative of human development that suggested a continual evolution and growth toward perfection in the human race. While modernity largely abandoned theological frameworks for understanding history, it still presupposed that we inhabit a "narratable world"[17] in which actions and events made sense as part of an ongoing story of human advance.

But as we entered the twentieth century, it became difficult to maintain that this self-authored story was really going to lead to a good end. Two World Wars, the Holocaust, Hiroshima, Vietnam, the Cold War, the killing fields of Cambodia, and the genocides in Bosnia and Rwanda drew the curtain on the Enlightenment faith in human progress. The myth of an inevitable advance lost credibility under the weight of evil and violence. The century that was, at its inception, called the "Christian century" turned out to be the deadliest century ever. Our trust that human beings could write for themselves a coherent story with a good ending collapsed. The result was not only an uncertainty about whether the human story would have a happy ending, but worse, a fear that our lives and our histories had no coherence at all. Having largely given up the belief that God guides the world's story, many began to wonder whether, in fact, the world had a story at all.

One characteristic of the postmodern turn at the end of the twentieth century has been a distrust in "metanarratives," the overarching stories (human or divine) that once provided a context for understanding our lives within a larger movement of history. These grand master stories (such as the biblical narrative or a story of national destiny) are often viewed with suspicion, seen as convenient fictions by which the powerful legitimate their domination. Many people have come to perceive their lives as a series of loosely connected singularities (like the rapidly juxtaposed and largely disconnected images in a music video). We find ourselves living amid the ruins of the modern project, trying to piece together a future when all we have are fragments from our past. It is not the case that in postmodernity chaos replaces order but that the two become indistinguishable. The secular view of time ushered in by the modern era continues to reign supreme, but now without the optimistic assumption that human beings could imprint order on its pristine sands. All moments become interchangeable.

Alongside the demise of the metanarrative came what some have called "the death of the subject." If there was one thing the modern era was sure about, it was the primacy of the subject, that is, the rational individual. All real knowledge had to pass the bar of one's individual reason and experience. But increasingly even personal identities, what we think we know and who we think we are, are experienced as fragmented, fluid, ever-changing, without anything like the stability and coherence of a "life story." Modernity gave us the idea that we could be self-creators, to be whatever we wanted to be apart from any identity given by family, culture, or even God. Yet we realized that a self-created self could always be re-created (move to a new city, buy a new car, find a new job, even get a new spouse). If my identity is not given in any significant way, then I can always become someone else. And so the stable, self-created subject of modernity is rapidly giving way to the fluid, unstable self of postmodernity. "From the standpoint of individualism," observes Alasdair MacIntyre, "I am what I myself choose to be. I can always, if I wish to, put in question what are taken to be the merely contingent social features of my existence."[18] MacIntyre adds that such a person is fated to be "a self that can have no history,"[19] and without history we become "unscripted, anxious stutterers in [our] actions as in [our] words."[20]

While some of this analysis of our present state can sound quite academic and abstract, the lived reality of the fragmented self is quite common. It is the everyday experience of compartmentalized people, whose work lives are disconnected from their home and church lives, whose public speech does not coincide with their private convictions, whose youth and old age sit uncomfortably as disjointed bookends to an autonomous adulthood. It is the everyday experience of ordinary people going out to "find themselves," people for whom self-creation has become their fate and their burden.

"There's No Point to Anything"—Or Is There?

Popular culture bears witness to this changing perception of self, story, and history. This is played out in the rise of nonnarrative media. MTV co-founder Bob Pittman notes that what was new about MTV was not just the widespread introduction of music videos to television but a new form of communication: "What we've introduced at MTV is nonnarrative form. . . . We rely on mood and emotion. We make you feel a certain way as opposed to you walking away with any particular knowledge."[21] It is one thing to create a nonnarrative music video; it is something more challenging to create a nonnarrative novel or a nonnarrative movie. Yet writers and movie makers have begun experimenting with storytelling that plays scenes out of sequence and reaches no resolution. As Robert Jenson has noted, "modernity has added a new genre of theater to the classic tragedy and comedy: the absurdist drama that displays precisely an absence of dramatic coherence."[22]

One of the central characters in the movie *Reality Bites* expresses just this sense of randomness and meaninglessness: "There's no point to anything. . . . It's all just a random lottery of meaningless tragedy in a series of near escapes."[23] The easy-going nihilism of this teen-angst movie gives way to thicker reflection on chaos, violence, narrative, and destiny in the film *Pulp Fiction*. The film plays its scenes out of order to create a sense of disruption and disorientation. Yet the story, once teased out and reconstructed, moves us to a point of asking whether God might have a plan for us and whether God might intervene in the apparent chaos of the world to call us out, or rather call us in, to a journey, a story, that is bigger than we are.

Samuel Jackson's character, Jules, miraculously (to his mind) escapes death when shots fired at him from close range inexplicably miss. Jules's partner, Vincent (played by John Travolta), refuses to believe that this is anything more than chance, a random bit of good luck. But Jules, convinced that he has "felt the hand of God," gives up his life as a hit man and goes forth, as he puts it, to wander the earth like Caine in the seventies TV series *Kung Fu*. The reference to "wandering like Caine," while initially offered as yet another Tarantino pop-culture reference, turns out to be a reference to a reference, since the Caine of *Kung Fu* already alludes to the biblical Cain, who wanders the earth as his punishment for murder. Jules, a killer like the biblical Cain, has apparently also been marked like Cain, so that he will not be killed in retaliation for his killing. So he goes forth not just to wander, but to quest for the good that he has undeservedly received. Vincent, refusing to see any higher purpose or divine plan, mocks Jules but ends up dead, a victim of the violence he had embraced.

Pulp Fiction, in its structure, provides a commentary on a world where metanarratives have become suspect, but despite all of its violence and gore, the film leaves us with an alternative to chaos and violence, and with a choice to be made. For even in the midst of a chaotic and violent world, the possibility exists that God is calling us into a story, a journey, in which our wandering will turn out to be less like the biblical Cain's and more like the wilderness wandering of the Israelites, who eventually crossed into the Promised Land. Maybe there is an author after all. Maybe our story—the world's story—can still have a good ending.

Telling an Old, Old Story—About Fear

No theological account of the "deep roots of fear" would be complete without a look at that foundational biblical story in which Adam and Eve first knew fear. In some ways all of our unhealthy fears are just new variations on this one fear, the fear that is flight from God.

The story of the "fall" of Adam and Eve is a story about human creatures unwilling to be creatures, who, like modern people, declared themselves self-creators. God created humankind, Genesis 1 tells us, in the image and likeness of God. Human beings were created for a life in community that mirrored the communal life of God as "three and one." We were made to image God as we lived and loved one another in the pattern of God's living and loving.

Yet human beings were not content with this derivative creaturely status, with the privilege and task of pointing beyond themselves to that which they imaged. Instead, they were tempted by the words of the serpent, the promise that they would "be like God" (Gen. 3:5). The change in status seems linguistically small—"imaging God" vs. "being like God"—but it is theologically vast: to reflect the goodness and beauty of God or to turn our gaze inward and claim goodness and beauty as our own. Instead of reflecting the light of God, human beings began to assert themselves as the source of light. And so we became unending self-creators, gods to ourselves.

It was when the first humans sought to be self-creators that they knew fear and hiding for the first time. After they had eaten of the forbidden tree, they heard God come into the garden, and they hid. "Where are you?" called God. Adam replied, "I heard the sound of you in the garden, and I was afraid, because I was naked; and I hid myself" (Gen. 3:9–10). Adam and Eve were afraid because they were naked, they were laid bare, transparent to each other and to God—a state of pure openness that should not have caused fear but which, to the human beings willing to transgress the boundaries of God, became a threat, since even the boundaries of their bodies no longer seemed secure.

No longer content to rest in the givenness of God's created order, human beings turned from being recipients of God's gifts to become masters and possessors of those gifts, claimants to the fruit, the knowledge, the power to determine good and evil, the power and burden to be god and not just reflect God. But because human beings were never made to be gods, we live with the uneasy truth that we cannot fulfill our divine aspirations. We fear failing as self-creators because we can only fail as self-creators. We fear death because we are not content to receive life as gift, and now with life in our hands we find ourselves incapable of sustaining it. We fear God's presence because God reminds us that we are not God.

The modern (and now the postmodern) world continues this primal flight from God, and so we live with fear—fear that can be stoked and manipulated by cruel events or greedy hucksters, but which is ultimately rooted in this age-old flight. We fear that our lives have no story because we have fled from the story God has given us. Our deep fears point us back to the deep story in which our flight from God leaves us fearful of a world that was meant to be received as gift. The "culture of fear" turns out not to be so new, but to be one more instance of our abiding human plight.

Notes

Chapter 1: Fear for Profit

1. Bono, "U2 Q&A on *How to Dismantle an Atomic Bomb*," Best Buy interview, online: http://www.bestbuy.com/site/olspage.jsp?id-pcmcat46100050008&type-category (accessed June 7, 2006).

2. Frank Furedi, *Paranoid Parenting* (Chicago: Chicago Review Press, 2002), 12.

3. Mark Peterzell, "A Message from the Chairman," American SIDS Institute, online: http://www.sids.org/ (accessed June 20, 2006).

4. *Finding Nemo,* DVD, directed by Andrew Stanton and Lee Unkrich (Buena Vista Pictures, 2003).

5. Susan T. Lennon, "That Little Freckle Could Be a Time Bomb," *Newsweek,* May 24, 2004, 14.

6. WYOU-TV 22, local CBS affiliate news, November 2, 2003, 11:00 edition.

7. Frank Furedi, *Culture of Fear,* rev. ed. (New York: Continuum, 2002), 6.

8. Centers for Disease Control, United States Statistics from 2002, online: http://www.cdc.gov/nchs/fastats/deaths.htm (accessed August 3, 2005).

9. See Furedi, *Culture of Fear,* 15–44.

10. Barry Glassner, *The Culture of Fear* (New York: Basic Books, 1999), 75.

11. Ibid., xi.

12. Ibid., 44.

13. Ibid., 44–45.

14. Ibid., xxii, from a Barbara Walters story on *20/20* in 1998.

15. Ibid., xxii.

16. Al Franken, *Lies and the Lying Liars Who Tell Them* (New York: Dutton, 2003), 1.

17. From NPR interview with Joseph Angotti, former senior vice president, NBC News, former executive producer, *NBC Nightly News with Tom Brokaw,* former vice president and executive producer, NBC News special programs, and now chair of the Broadcast Department at Medill School of Journalism, Northwestern University, in Rick Karr, "Moore Film Targets Gun Violence, American Media," *All*

Things Considered, November 2, 2002, online: http://www.npr.org/templates/story/story.php?storyId=829697 (accessed October 16, 2006).

18. Karr, "Moore Film Targets Gun Violence."

19. Joseph Angotti in Karr, "Moore Film Targets Gun Violence."

20. See for instance the account in Ron Suskind, *The One Percent Doctrine* (New York: Simon and Schuster, 2006), 24–26, 64.

21. George W. Bush, State of the Union address, 2003, online: http://www.white house.gov/news/releases/2003/01/20030128-19.html (accessed October 29, 2003); Christopher Marquis, "The Struggle for Iraq: Diplomacy: Powell Admits No Hard Proof in Linking Iraq to Al Qaeda," *New York Times,* January 9, 2004, A10.

22. See Colin Powell's admission in Marquis, "Struggle for Iraq."

23. Dana Milbank, "Bush Disavows Hussein-Sept. 11 Link," *Washington Post,* September 18, 2003, A18.

24. Bill Clinton, "Address to Democratic National Convention," 2004, online: http://www.americanrhetoric.com/speeches/convention2004/billclinton2004dnc.htm (accessed September 4, 2006).

25. Glassner, *Culture of Fear,* 45–46.

26. Bishop Paul V. Marshall, "Does God Want Us to Hate Anyone on His Behalf?" *Morning Call,* October 2003, http://www.diobeth.org/ Bishop/Secular/sec74.html (accessed October 16, 2003).

27. http://www.feargod.com/feargod.htm (accessed August 3, 2005).

28. Spencer Burke, *Making Sense of Church* (Grand Rapids: Zondervan, 2003), 129.

29. See John Fischer's discussion of this in *Fearless Faith* (Eugene, OR: Harvest House, 2002).

30. Hans Urs von Balthasar, *The Christian and Anxiety* (San Francisco: Ignatius Press, 2000), 35.

31. Richard Hays, *The Moral Vision of the New Testament* (New York: Harper Collins, 1996), 197.

32. Ibid.

Chapter 2: Fear and the Moral Life

1. Simon Harak, *Virtuous Passions* (Mahwah, NJ: Paulist Press, 1993), 2.

2. Ibid., 22–22.

3. Walter Brueggemann, "The Liturgy of Abundance, the Myth of Scarcity," *Christian Century,* March 24–31, 1999, online: http://www.religion-online.org/show article.asp?title=533 (accessed June 12, 2006).

4. H. Richard Niebuhr, *The Responsible Self* (San Francisco: HarperSanFrancisco, 1963), 60.

5. Ibid., 140.

6. Dashboard Confessional, "The Places You Have Come to Fear the Most," *The Places You Have Come to Fear the Most* (Vagrant Records, 2001).

7. Dashboard Confessional, "This Ruined Puzzle," *The Places You Have Come to Fear the Most* (Vagrant Records, 2001).

8. Thomas Aquinas, trans. Fathers of the English Dominican Province, *Summa Theologica,* I–II (Allen, TX: Christian Classics, 1948), Q. 44, art.1.

9. See Aquinas, *Summa,* I–II, Q. 65, art. 5; Westminster Shorter Catechism, Q. 1.

10. Frank Furedi, *Culture of Fear,* rev. ed. (New York: Continuum, 2002), 147.

11. Ibid.

12. Ibid., 69.

13. Ibid., 25.

14. Ibid., citing M. Hillman, J. Adams, and J. Whiteleg, *One False Move . . . A Study of Children's Independent Mobility* (London: PSI Publishing, 1990), 111.

15. Daniel Schorr, "Week in Review with Daniel Schorr," *Weekend Edition Saturday,* January 10, 2004, online: http://216.35.21.77/templates/story.php?storyld-1592241 (accessed January 19, 2004).

16. George W. Bush, "Remarks by the President at 2002 Graduation Exercise of the United States Military Academy, West Point, New York," online: http://www.whitehouse.gov/news/releases/2002/06/20020601-3.html, posted June 1, 2002 (accessed February 2, 2004).

17. George W. Bush, *National Security Strategy of the United States of America,* online: http://www.whitehouse.gov/nsc/nssall.html, posted: September 17, 2002 (accessed February 2, 2004).

18. Jon Ungoed-Thomas and David Leppard, "Shoot-to-Kill without Warning," *London Times,* July 31, 2005.

19. Jane Kirby, "Archbishop Warns against 'Drastic' Anti-Terror Measures," The Press Association Limited, July 30, 2005.

Chapter 3: Why Fearlessness Is a Bad Idea

1. For an account of this story see Jacob and Wilhelm Grimm, "The Story of a Boy Who Went Forth to Learn Fear," online: http://www.pitt.edu/~dash/grimm004.html (accessed January 3, 2005).

2. Aquinas, *Summa,* II–II, Q. 19, art. 3.

3. Ibid., Q. 126, art. 1.

4. Karl Barth, *Church Dogmatics*, vol. 3, part 3, ed. G. W. Bromiley and T. F. Torrance, trans. G. W. Bromiley and R. J. Ehrlich (Edinburgh: T & T Clark, 1960), 295ff.

5. Augustine, *The Confessions,* trans. Maria Boulding, OSB (New York: Random House, 1997), bk. IV, 59.

6. Ibid., 62.

7. Ibid., 63.

8. Cited in Corey Robin, *Fear: The History of a Political Idea* (Oxford: Oxford University Press, 2004), 132.

9. Aquinas, *Summa,* I–II, Q. 44, art. 4.

10. Benedict, *Rule of St. Benedict,* ch. 4, online: http://www.kansasmonks.org/RuleOfStBenedict.html#ch4 (accessed June 1, 2006).

11. Joseph Cardinal Bernardin, *The Gift of Peace* (New York: Doubleday, 1997), 93.

12. Ibid., 109.

13. Ellen Davis, *Getting Involved with God: Rediscovering the Old Testament* (Cambridge, MA: Cowley Press, 2001), 102.

14. Ibid., 102–3.

15. Ibid., 103.

16. Shmuley Boteach, *Face Your Fear* (New York: St. Martin's Press, 2004), 8.

17. Aquinas, *Summa,* II–II, Q. 126, art. 1.

18. George W. Bush, State of the Union address, 2005, online: http://www.whitehouse.gov/news/releases/2005/02/20050202-11.html/ (accessed September 8, 2006).

19. *Star Wars: Episode I—The Phantom Menace,* written and directed by George Lucas (20th Century Fox and Lucasfilm Ltd., 1999).

20. Ibid.

21. U2, "Peace on Earth," *All That You Can't Leave Behind* (Interscope Records, 2000).

Chapter 4: Putting Fear in Its Place

1. Michelle Malkin, "Candidates Ignore 'Security Moms,' at Their Peril," *USA Today,* July 21, 2004, final ed., A11.

2. Aquinas, *Summa,* I–II, Q. 42, art. 3.

3. Following Aristotle, who said, "Of the faults that are committed one consists in fearing what one should not, another in fearing as we should not, another in fearing when we should not, and so on." Aristotle, *Nicomachean Ethics,* bk. III, ch. 7, online: http://classics.mit.edu/Aristotle/nicomachaen.3.iii.html (accessed February 2, 2004).

4. Aquinas, *Summa,* I–II, Q. 42, art. 2.

5. George Gerbner, "Reclaiming Our Cultural Mythology," *In Context,* vol. 38, Spring 1994, online: http://www.context.org/ICLIB/IC38/Gerbner.htm (accessed September 8, 2006).

6. Ron Suskind, *The One Percent Doctrine* (New York: Simon and Schuster, 2006), 62.

7. Ibid.

8. Aquinas, *Summa,* II–II, Q. 19, art. 3.

9. Ibid., Q. 125, art. 2.

10. Ibid., art. 1.

11. Aquinas, *Summa,* I–II, Q. 43, art. 2.

12. Ibid., II–II, Q.125, art. 4.

13. Ibid.

14. As Aquinas puts it, joy "is caused by love, either through the presence of the thing loved, or because the proper good of the thing loved exists and endures in it; and the latter is the case chiefly in the love of benevolence, whereby a man rejoices in the well-being of his friend, though he be absent." Aquinas, *Summa,* II–II, Q. 28, art. 1.

15. Hans Urs von Balthasar, *The Christian and Anxiety,* trans. Dennis D. Martin and Michael J. Miller (San Francisco: Ignatius Press, 2000), 88.

16. Dietrich Bonhoeffer, *The Cost of Discipleship,* rev. ed., trans. R. H. Fuller (New York: Macmillan, 1963), 99.

17. David Ford, *The Shape of Living* (Grand Rapids: Baker, 1997).

18. Ibid., 17.

19. Ibid., 66.

Chapter 5: Community and Courage

1. Frank Furedi, *Culture of Fear,* rev. ed. (New York: Continuum, 2002), 67–68.

2. Ibid., 172.

3. "Taizé: A Lifelong Commitment," online: http://www.taize.fr/en_article6.html (accessed February 24, 2006).

4. Otto Selles, "Taizé in the Fall: A Parable of Community," *Books and Culture,* November 29, 2005, online: http://www.christianitytoday.com/books/features/bc corner/051128.html (accessed February 24, 2006).

5. Aristotle, *Nichomachean Ethics,* trans. W. D. Ross, in Richard McKeon, ed., *Introduction to Aristotle* (New York: Random House, 1947), III.7, 363.

6. Paul J. Wadell, *Friendship and the Moral Life* (Notre Dame, IN: University of Notre Dame Press, 1989), xiii.

7. John Milbank, *Theology and Social Theory: Beyond Secular Reason* (Oxford and Cambridge, MA: Basil Blackwell, 1990), 411.

8. See Claude Payne and Hamilton Beazley, *Reclaiming the Great Commission* (New York: Jossey-Bass, 2000).

9. Yan Martel, *Life of Pi* (Orlando: Harcourt, 2001), 161–62.

10. Wadell, *Friendship and the Moral Life*, 164.

Chapter 6: Narrative and Providence

1. John Calvin, *Institutes of the Christian Religion,* ed. John T. McNeill, trans. Ford Lewis Battles (Philadelphia: Westminster Press, 1960), I.17.10.

2. Ibid., I.17.11.

3. The following paragraphs draw on Langdon Gilkey's helpful analysis of the demise of providence in modernity. Langdon Gilkey, "The Concept of Providence in Contemporary Theology," *Journal of Religion* 43:3 (July 1963): 171–92.

4. Quoted in Barbara Brown Taylor, *God in Pain* (Nashville: Abingdon Press, 1998), 106.

5. Ibid., 106–107.

6. Erich Auerbach, *Mimesis* (Princeton, NJ: Princeton University Press, 1953), 73–74.

7. Ibid.

8. Ibid., 74.

9. Ibid., 317.

10. See Michael Goldberg, *Why Should Jews Survive?* (New York: Oxford University Pres, 1995), for such a reading of Jewish history as well as a helpful discussion of the role of the "master story" in religious traditions.

11. Hans Frei, *The Identity of Jesus Christ* (Philadelphia: Fortress Press, 1975), 161.

12. Elie Wiesel, *Night* (New York Bantam Books, 1982), 42.

13. Samuel Wells, *Improvisation: The Drama of Christian Ethics* (Grand Rapids: Brazos Press, 2004).

14. Ibid., 57.

15. Flannery O'Connor, *The Habit of Being* (New York: Farrar, Straus, and Giroux, 1988), 57.

Chapter 7: Security and Vulnerability

1. David Daily, personal correspondence, April 14, 1999.

2. Augustine, *Confessions,* trans. Maria Boulding (New York: Random House, 1997), 73–74.

3. Craig Whitlock, "At Auschwitz, Pope Invokes a 'Heartfelt Cry,'" *Washington Post,* May 29, 2006, p. A14, online: http://www.washingtonpost.com/wp-dyn/content/article/2006/05/28/AR2006052800453.html (accessed May 29, 2006).

4. For what follows see Samuel Wells, *Improvisation: The Drama of Christian Ethics* (Grand Rapids: Brazos Press, 2004, 103–42.

5. Ibid., 134.

6. Goldberg, *Why Should Jews Survive?* 3–17.

7. Wells provides an interesting discussion of "reincorporation" in *Improvisation,* 143–53.

8. Ibid., 110.

Chapter 8: The Risk of Hospitality

1. C. S. Lewis, *The Lion, the Witch, and the Wardrobe* (New York: Macmillan, 1950), 75–76.

2. Marc Schultz, "Dangerous Reading," *weeklyplanet.com*, July 17, 2003, online: http://www.weeklyplanet.com/gyrobase/Content?oid=oid%3A2838 (accessed May 26, 2006).

3. *Fahrenheit 9/11*, DVD, directed by Michael Moore (2004; Columbia Tri-Star Home Entertainment, 2004).

4. Zygmunt Bauman, *Community: Seeking Safety in an Insecure World* (Malden, MA: Blackwell, Polity Press, 2001), 1–2.

5. Ibid., 2.

6. Ibid., 145.

7. Philip D. Kenneson and James L. Street, *Selling Out the Church: The Dangers of Church Marketing* (Nashville: Abingdon, 1997), 21.

8. Ibid., 88–106.

9. Kay Keenan and Roy Tripp, "Why Grow, Why Now," Grow Your Church Now, 2006. This is a workbook produced and distributed by the authors at their Grow Your Church Now seminars.

10. Brian McLaren, *More Ready Than You Realize* (Grand Rapids: Zondervan, 2002), 137–40.

11. Christine D. Pohl, *Making Room: Recovering Hospitality as a Christian Tradition* (Grand Rapids: Eerdmans, 1999), 141.

12. Ibid., 136.

13. Adalbert deVogüé, *The Rule of Saint Benedict: A Doctrinal and Spiritual Commentary*, trans. J. B. Hasbrouck (Kalamazoo: Cistercian Publications, 1983), 261–62; cited in Pohl, *Recovering Hospitality*, 139.

14. Dan Harris, "Man on a Mission," on ABC News, *Guilt or Innocence?* June 22, 2006.

15. Fr. Andrew Gerns, rector, Trinity Episcopal Church, Easton, PA, personal correspondence, used by permission.

16. David Ford, *The Modern Theologians* (Malden, MA: Blackwell, 1997), 727.

17. All quotes are from *Pieces of April*, DVD, directed by Peter Hedges (2003; MGM Home Entertainment, 2004).

18. Pohl, *Making Room*, xiii.

19. Ibid., 13.

Chapter 9: The Risk of Peacemaking

1. Mary Pope Osborne, *Summer of the Sea Serpent* (New York: Random House, 2004), 81–86.

2. Episcopal Church, 75th General Convention, Resolution D020, "End the War in Iraq," online: http://gc2006.org/legislation/view_leg_detail.aspx?id=252&type=CURRENT (accessed June 27, 2006).

3. Monks of the Weston Priory (Benedictines), "Statement From Benedictine Men & Women on the Preparations for War," October 12, 2002, online: http://www.westonpriory.org/101202statement.html (accessed August 18, 2005).

4. Douglas John Hall, "The Mystery of God's Dominion," in *God and the Nations* (Minneapolis: Fortress Press, 1995), 23.

5. John L. O'Sullivan, *New York Morning News,* December 27, 1845, cited in Walter A. McDougall, *Promised Land, Crusader State: The American Encounter with the World since 1776* (New York: Houghton Mifflin, 1997), 84.

6. John M. Blum et al. *The National Experience: A History of the United States,* 6th ed. (New York: Harcourt Brace Jovanovich, 1985), 276, cited in Michael T. Lubragge, "Manifest Destiny: The Philosophy That Created a Nation," online: http://www.let .rug.nl/usa/E/manifest/manif1.htm#coi (accessed June 2, 2006).

7. Senator Albert J. Beveridge, "In Support of an American Empire," U.S. Senate, Washington, DC, January 9, 1900, *Record,* 56 Cong., I Sess., 704–12, online: http:// www.mtholyoke.edu/acad/intrel/ajb72.htm (accessed June 2, 2006).

8. Ibid.

9. Senator Albert J. Beveridge, "The March of the Flag," campaign speech, September 16, 1898, online: http://www.fordham.edu/halsall/mod/1898beveridge .html (accessed June 1, 2006).

10. George W. Bush, "State of the Union," January 28, 2003, online: http:// www.whitehouse.gov/news/releases/2003/01/20030128-19.html (accessed June 7, 2006).

11. George W. Bush, "State of the Union," January 20, 2004, online: http:// www.whitehouse.gov/news/releases/2004/01/20040120-7.html (accessed June 7, 2006).

12. T. S. Eliot, *Murder in the Cathedral* (New York: Harcourt Brace Jovanovich, 1935), 73.

13. Ibid., 69.

14. Ibid., 70.

15. T. S. Eliot, *Four Quartets* (New York: Harcourt Brace Jovanovich, 1943), 56, 57, 59.

16. The following story comes from Sue Scott, "Blessed Are the Young Peacemakers," *Sharing,* Winter 1998, reprinted at Peacemaker Ministries, online: http:// bookstore.peacemaker.net/html/truc12.htm (accessed September 27, 2006).

17. Ibid.

18. Ibid.

19. Ibid.

20. Daniel M. Bell Jr., "Just War as Christian Discipleship," The Ekklesia Project, Pamphlet #14 (Eugene, OR: Wipf and Stock, 2005), 11.

21. Ibid., 20.

22. Jérôme Bindé, "Toward an Ethics of the Future," *Public Culture* 12:1 (2000): 52.

23. Bell, "Just War as Christian Discipleship," 20

24. "Statement by Alabama Clergymen," April 12, 1963, online: http://www .stanford.edu/group/King//frequentdocs/clergy.pdf (accessed June 6, 2006).

25. Martin Luther King Jr., "Letter from Birmingham Jail," 1963, online: http:// www.almaz.com/nobel/peace/MLK-jail.html (accessed June 6, 2006).

26. Martin Luther King Jr., "I Have a Dream," 1963, online: http://www.uscon stitution.net/dream.html (accessed June 6, 2006).

27. Ibid.

28. Martin Luther King Jr. "Where Do We Go from Here?" 1967, online: http:// www.princeton.edu/pr/mlk/journey.html (accessed June 6, 2006).

Chapter 10: The Risk of Generosity

1. BBC News, "Secret CIA Jail Claims Rejected," online: http://news.bbc.co.uk/2/ hi/europe/5056614.stm (accessed June 8, 2006).

2. Ibid.

3. Walter Brueggemann, "Enough Is Enough," *The Other Side,* November–December 2001, online: http://jmm.aaa.net.au/articles/1181.htm (accessed June 14, 2006).

4. Aquinas, *Summa,* II–II, Q. 125, art. 4.

5. Adam Smith, *The Wealth of Nations,* Modern Library ed. (New York: Random House, 1947), 423.

6. Adam Smith, *Theory of Moral Sentiments,* 6th ed., IV.1.10. online: http://www.econlib.org/library/Smith/smMS.html (accessed June 12, 2006).

7. Ibid.

8. Ibid.

9. John Milbank, *Theology and Social Theory: Beyond Secular Reason* (Oxford and Cambridge, MA: Basil Blackwell, 1990), 29.

10. Ibid.

11. Max Weber, *The Protestant Ethic and the Spirit of Capitalism,* trans. Talcott Parsons (New York: Routledge, 1992), 177.

12. The following paragraphs draw on Walter Brueggemann, "The Liturgy of Abundance, the Myth of Scarcity," *Christian Century,* March 24–31, 1999, online: http://www.religion-online.org/showarticle.asp?title=533 (accessed June 12, 2006).

13. Ibid.

14. Ibid.

15. Christopher Franks, "Thomas's Economics and the Redundancy of Natural Law," paper presented at The Society of Christian Ethics Annual Meeting, January 2004.

16. John Calvin, *Institutes of the Christian Religion,* ed. John T. McNeill, trans. Ford Lewis Battles (Philadelphia: Westminster Press, 1960), III.vii.5, 695.

17. Ibid., III.vii.8, 698.

18. Ibid.

19. This reading comes from a sermon preached by Bob Dunham at University Presbyterian Church.

20. *American Beauty,* DVD, directed by Sam Mendes (DreamWorks, 1999).

21. Pura Vida Coffee, "Mission Statement," online: http://www.puravidacoffee.com/work/work_mission.asp (accessed June 14, 2006).

22. Craigslist, "craigslist factsheet," May 2006, online: http://www.craigslist.org/about/pr/factsheet.html(accessed June 14, 2006).

23. Craig Newmark, interview with Nate Kaiser, nPost.com, online: http://www.craigslist.org/about/press/npostinterview.html (accessed June 7, 2006).

24. Rachel E. Silverman, "Ranking Job Boards," *Wall Street Journal,* April 25, 2000, online: http://www.craigslist.org/about/press/rankingjobboards.html (accessed June 14, 2006).

25. Craigslist, "craigslist Factsheet."

26. Matt Richtel, "Craig's To-Do List: Leave Millions on the Table," *New York Times,* September 6, 2004, online: http://www.craigslist.org/about/press/leave.millions.html (accessed June 7, 2006).

27. Ibid.

28. Ibid.

29. Craigslist, "Craigslist Is About," online: http://www.craigslist.org/about/mission.and.history.html (accessed June 15, 2006).

30. Craigslist, "A Little History," online: http://www.craigslist.org/about/mission.and.history.html (accessed June 7, 2006).

31. Craig Newmark, "Leonard Cohen on Fresh Air," blog post, posted May 22, 2006, online: http://www.cnewmark.com/archives/000611.html (accessed June 7, 2006).

32. Craig Newmark, personal e-mail correspondence, June 13, 2006, used by permission.

33. Brueggemann, "Enough Is Enough."

Appendix: The Deep Roots of Fear

1. William T. Cavanaugh, *Theopolitical Imagination* (London: T & T Clark, 2002), 20–31.

2. Quoted in Richard S. Peters, "Introduction" to Thomas Hobbes, *Leviathan,* ed. Michael Oakeshott (New York: Macmillan, 1962), 7.

3. Ibid.

4. Hobbes, *Leviathan*, 100.

5. Hobbes, *De Cive*, I.1.1.

6. Judith Shklar, "The Liberalism of Fear," in Nancy L. Rosenblum, ed., *Liberalism and the Moral Life* (Cambridge: Harvard University Press, 1989), 29.

7. Judith Shklar, "Putting Cruelty First," *Daedalus* 111:3, Summer 1982, 17–28, online: http://www.democratiya.com/review.asp?reviews_id=24 (accessed June 21, 2006).

8. Judith Shklar, "A Life of Learning," American Council of Learned Societies, Occasional Paper, no. 9, Charles Homer Haskins Lecture for 1989, online: http://www.acls.org/op9.htm (accessed June 21, 2006).

9. Ibid.

10. Ibid.

11. Ibid.

12. Corey Robin, *Fear: The History of a Political Idea* (Oxford: Oxford University Press, 2004), 3.

13. Ibid., 249.

14. Ibid., 164.

15. Ibid.

16. The following paragraphs draw on Robert Jenson's argument in "How the World Lost Its Story," *First Things* 36 (October 1993), 19–24, online: http://www.firstthings.com/ftissues/ft9310/articles/jenson.html (accessed May 18, 2005).

17. Jenson, "How the World Lost Its Story."

18. Alasdair MacIntyre, *After Virtue,* 2nd ed. (Notre Dame, IN: University of Notre Dame Press, 1984), 220.

19. Ibid., 221.

20. Ibid., 216.

21. Quoted in Craig Detweiler and Barry Taylor, *A Matrix of Meanings* (Grand Rapids: Baker, 2003), 34.

22. Jenson, "How the World Lost Its Story."

23. *Reality Bites,* directed by Ben Stiller (Universal City Studios, 1994), quoted in Richard Winter, *Still Bored in a Culture of Entertainment* (Downers Grove, IL: InterVarsity Press, 2002), 90.